BOSS RULE

"The candidates selected were not to be left out on a limb, so to speak, to finance and run their own separate campaigns, but the City Charter Committee was to organize completely in wards and precincts to elect them, and run one main campaign for them all.

That was an epochal decision. At the time it seemed a natural result to reach, growing out of long discussion and preliminary decisions as questions arose. But it represented a political method theretofore unknown in municipal reform, and it marks the most distinctive feature of the whole Cincinnati experiment. If we have contributed anything to the permanent good of our nation, politically speaking, it is this plan, rather than the service of any particular individual."

CHARLES P. TAFT in *City Management: The Cincinnati Experiment*, page 76.

>>> >>>·<<< <<<

SHALLOW: Well conceited, Davy. About the business, Davy.

DAVY: I beseech you, sir, to countenance William Visor against Clement Perkes of the hill.

SHALLOW: There are many complaints, Davy, against that Visor; that Visor is an arrant knave, on my knowledge.

DAVY: I grant your worship that he is a knave, sir; but yet, God forbid, sir, but a knave should have some countenance at his friend's request. An honest man, sir is able to speak for himself, when a knave is not. I have served your worship truly sir, this eight years; and if I cannot once or twice in a quarter bear out a knave against an honest man, I have little credit with your worship. The knave is mine honest friend, sir; therefore, I beseech your worship, let him be countenanced.

SHALLOW: Go to; I say, he shall have no wrong.

Henry IV, Part II; Act V; Scene I.

BOSS RULE

PORTRAITS IN CITY POLITICS

By J. T. SALTER

ASSOCIATE PROFESSOR OF POLITICAL
SCIENCE, UNIVERSITY OF WISCONSIN

New York WHITTLESEY HOUSE *London*

McGRAW-HILL BOOK COMPANY, INC.

PUBLISHED BY WHITTLESEY HOUSE
A divison of the McGraw-Hill Book Company, Inc.

For

KATHARINE

✩

NOTE

➤➤➤ ➤➤➤ ➤➤≪≪ ≪≪ ≪≪

MORE than 90 per cent of my total materials—only a fraction are used in this present volume—have been taken from the lips of people rather than from printed documents, and my list of acknowledgments is necessarily a long one. The names that are listed here, however, are only a few of those that have contributed to my work—some of my most valuable insights and facts have come from individuals who do not want their identity disclosed. Other persons will not be thanked here because of space limitations. Toward both groups I feel deepest gratitude. I am especially indebted to my former students (native Philadelphians) at the University of Pennsylvania. They gave me my first close contact with the Philadelphia organization, and on my return to this city they personally presented me to the politicians. Messrs. Clarence M. Freedman and P. Morton Rothberg come first to mind, although Mr. D. Barlow Burke and more than thirty other students provided introductions and guides that were valuable beyond reckoning. The politician himself was most generous with his time and helpful in his interest. So much of my material comes from him that this is in a special sense his book. I am also truly conscious of the honor of membership conferred upon me by those outstanding citizens—members of the Philadelphia Committee of Public Affairs. Their weekly discussions were invaluable in continually giving me the other side of the picture in politics. Professors James T. Young of the University of Pennsylvania and Robert C. Brooks of Swarthmore College; Mr. T. Henry Walnut, and Dr. A. E. Miller of Philadelphia merit my warmest thanks for their encouragement and helpful questions and comments at various stages of my work. I also especially thank Miss Marie Martel, the Hon. Clinton Rogers Woodruff, Professor Brooke Graves of Temple University, Dr. David H. Kurtzman, Mr. Jacob Silverman, Mr. William C. Beyer, director of the Bureau of Municipal Research of Philadelphia, Mr. William T. Bissell of New York City, and Mr. John Davis of Washington, D. C., for ideas and information generously given. To Miss Ruth Wallerstein of the University of Wisconsin, I am deeply grateful for most revealing comments on different sections of my manuscript which she so kindly read. To my colleague, Professor Llewellyn Pfankucken, and my onetime assistant, Miss Mary C. Trackett of the University of Wisconsin, I give my best thanks. Miss Ann Mallon of Jenkintown provided me with most adequate secretarial service. The fellowships given me by the Social Science Research Council provided me with needed funds for carrying on my research in Philadelphia. I am most grateful for this aid. I also wish to express my thanks to the University of Wisconsin for a leave of absence which permitted me to devote an entire year to my investigation. To Katharine Shepard Hayden my obligation is

NOTE

greatest; we have talked countless hours about different questions pertinent to this book. Her intelligent interest, caustic criticism, and wise suggestions have contributed more to it than I can briefly say.

I am grateful to the editors of the *Yale Review*, *Harper's Magazine*, the *American Mercury*, *Revue de Sciences Politiques*, *North American Review*, the *American Political Science Review*, the *National Municipal Review*, the *Dalhousie Review*, the *General Magazine and Historical Chronicle*, and the *Oberlin Alumni Magazine* for their generous permission to reprint with slight modification some of the materials contained in this volume.

In spite of the fact that this manuscript has been read by politicians, independents, and professors, there may be error in it. If there is, I humbly apologize and accept the full responsibility.

J. T. SALTER.

MADISON, WISCONSIN,
April, 1935.

CONTENTS

BOSS RULE

INTRODUCTION

WHETHER the reader lives in Maine, Louisiana, or Oregon, he can learn much about the nature of the party organizations and politicians in his own state by considering the organization and men herein described. The cardinal principles underlying all party organization and the functional traits of all politicians are the same; it is only the party labels that differ. (And to the professional politician even this party label is not so meaningful as to prevent a Democratic boss in Chicago or elsewhere from helping a Republican boss in the same locality. There is likely to be a see-sawing back and forth of jobs and other favors among bosses—a tendency to observe the golden rule. The future is long and the next election is always near at hand. Each boss controls what all bosses need—votes. In many places the boss's opponent is not another boss, but an independent, a reformer.) Tammany has been Democratic for more than a century—since its beginning in 1791; and the powerful Pendergast organization in Kansas City is also Democratic. It happens that the dominant party organization in Philadelphia is Republican. The strongest party organizations in Chicago, San Francisco, New Orleans, Indianapolis, Lexington, Boston, or Baltimore may be

3

ostensibly either Democratic or Republican, but, not-withstanding the party label on their banner, their method of wooing the sovereign voter is everywhere the same. And although I write of urban politicians, concrete individuals whom I know in the flesh, I find that, when I look at them singly, I see salient characteristics of the norm for all politicians. Those who devote their lives to the garnering of votes in the mountains of Kentucky or among the Norwegians of Dane County in Wisconsin have much in common with their counterparts in the city of Penn and Vare.

There are differences, it is true—differences resulting from varied economic conditions, cultural traditions, geographical situations, personality factors, and a changing *Zeitgeist*. Men are sometimes killed on election day in Bloody Breathitt County, Kentucky. No one has been murdered in an election feud in Dane County within the memory of men now living. The most recent election murder in Philadelphia occurred in 1917. And political addresses are more frequently given by winning candidates for public offices in Wisconsin than in Pennsylvania. But the identifying traits of politicians and the fundamental attributes of their constituencies conform pretty largely to a standard behavior pattern. If ballots have not so completely proved a substitute for bullets in the southern highlands as they have in the plain country elsewhere, this is merely an added descriptive fact concerning the mores of a people in a particular area. Or if solid (and specious?) argument counts for much in political contests in the Badger State, this statement must be included in any vital description

4

of politics in Wisconsin. The identifying facts concerning one aspect of politics in two widely different areas are additions to rather than substitutions for the basic traits of politicians and their political organizations.

First of all I propose to write briefly of party organizations—because everywhere they have a sameness most remarkable for a country in which the framework of the official city governments, for example, is so varied. An explanation of this may be found in the significant fact that the framework of official governments is an artificial legal device, based on abstract theory, historical incident, and fancied or real imitation; while the party organizations themselves are a natural product, created to meet a given need. They began functioning before the law was technically aware of their existence; and they have drawn their life and power from the realities in the political process. In short, the organizations of the major parties in the United States are practically the same wherever they are found, because their subject matter—human nature in politics—is a constant.

The largest territorial units in the United States are the separate forty-eight states. Each of these states selects one man and one woman to serve on a national committee of each of the two major parties. The national committee, like the United States Senate, is composed of the most powerful politicians in the country or their representatives. This committee is at the apex of the party structure, and is so powerful that it has been called the "President Maker."

This structure is a pyramid with a hierarchy of party committees ranging from the national committee down to the party workers in the unit cell of the party structure—the precinct. There are about 120,000 of these precincts in the United States. (For example, there are 5,000 of them in New York City, 3,000 in Chicago, and 1,283 in Philadelphia.) The precincts spread out over our 125,000,000 people like a finely meshed net. This party net is of unequal strength and fineness, and is strongest and most closely woven in great urban centers. Even here, however, in actuality it is not of an even texture, and it is powerful only when it has much work to perform. This greatest work is found among people that cannot manage their own affairs—the poor and ignorant, the socially handicapped groups.

In sparsely settled areas the smallest territorial division represented by a party committee is apt to be a township (there are 20,000 of them); in urban areas it is a precinct, ward, or city. Theoretically there is a party committee for every territorial district that elects a candidate to public office, but actually the existence and functioning of a party committee depend on the traditions of a people in a given section and its density of population.

Without considering the committees ranging between the national committee at the apex and the precinct committee at the base of the party pyramid, I shall merely say that there is a varying and ill-defined, though often very real, relation existing between one committee and the committees immediately below and above it. Thus in place of the check and balance system in the party structure there is a pyramiding of influence. A member of a precinct committee may also be a member of

6

a ward, county, or state committee; or, what more often happens, there will be some one on the committee who is the personal choice of a more powerful member on a higher committee.

Battles are won or lost (barring the great depression years like 1932-?, when a tide overwhelmed party workers never before beaten) in a precinct. This precinct organization may be made up of one or two individual leaders or workers, or there may be a small committee. In either case, however, there is one person that is "the" leader, and the other individuals are his helpers, co-workers, or, possibly, in times of stress, his opponents. These leaders meet the voters face to face and live in the territory that they represent. They are either elected by the direct vote of the party members as in Philadelphia, or appointed by the ward leader as in Chicago. But in any case, there is a close relation between the leaders in the precincts and the leaders in a ward, a relation as close as that between the interested members of a single family.

The statement that there are identifying personality traits common to all politicians is obvious to some and difficult to explain to others. It is somewhat like saying that all soldiers are the same and then realizing that there is only one General Pershing to some hundreds of thousands of other men wearing a military uniform. Even in the army, however, it is reasonable to believe that in the case of either a brigadier-general or an enlisted man in the rear rank each has a certain point of view— the professional's attitude—toward peace and war, life and death—a certain outlook on the world that

7

sets off the man wearing a uniform from the rest of us.

The politician, too, has a professional outlook toward politics. Whether he is Senator LaFollette or the lowliest ward heeler in McNutt's machine in Indiana—a machine with a very real powerhouse—he has an attitude or feeling for campaigns and elections that can be experienced only by the gentry who have sought election at the hands of the people over a period of years. Just as a student cannot become a lawyer by reading one book, nor a physician by performing one laboratory experiment, neither can a citizen become a politician (in the sense in which the term is used in this book) by successfully campaigning in one election. Time, seasoned with experience, is required, even as it is required in the work of any artist or professional man. (The true politician is something of both.)

All politicians (as I shall say many times) serve the people—or seem to. This service function is the *raison d'être* of everyone who asks for support at the polls, whether he be President Roosevelt or Bathhouse John Coughlin of Chicago. In the case of the former the service may be "public," applying to all persons similarly situated, whereas with the ward politician the service is most likely to be private and personal. But votes are invariably cast because the voter has received, or expects to receive, service, or service's worth. This service may be an old-age pension law, a tariff, or merely a friendly smile.

Politicians are likely to have political "it"—a pungent personality that captures attention amid the

8

rush and tumult of daily living. Al Smith has it; Herbert Hoover has not, nor did Calvin Coolidge have it. All young motion-picture stars who are notably successful do not have "it" (here meaning sex appeal—not political appeal); but the great majority have—and so it is with politicians.

Politicians are avid and often good talkers—if not publicly, then privately. The successful ones in Wisconsin, for example, are arguers or debaters as well. They are usually men who can plead their cases before a large group of people. However, politicians in other sections of the country may or may not be able to speak effectively to more than a handful of people at a time. The inability to speak convincingly to a large group of people is characteristic of some of the strongest ward leaders that I know. But even though this inability to speak compellingly before a numerous assembly is a handicap, yet it is not a fatal one. O'Brien in New York City was vanquished by the Seabury probe and the depression—not by his inability to talk.

Politicians are men and women of infinite variety and no two are the same. The successful ones, however, are those that (1) stick everlastingly at it, (2) know that the kingdom of heaven is taken by violence, (3) live decades among their people and learn to judge their wants, (4) have a flair for getting along with people, (5) have problem-solving ability, and (6) understand that politics is the science of the possible. Of course it goes without saying that a United States Senator or the governor of a state has something that a ward politician lacks—something that may be briefly described as vision.

9

(A Senator can see over an entire state while a ward politician's vision is limited to a precinct or a ward.) But a Senator who is standing on his own feet (that is, one who has not been appointed by some more powerful politician) is probably a ward politician writ large; acquiring a knowledge of the party workers in the ward is the surest way of learning the basic facts about the enormously important subject of realistic politics.

And finally it may be added that in temperament politicians are more apt to be like an Aaron Burr than a John Quincy Adams; and furthermore, it cannot be said of politicians, as is so often remarked of other arresting personalities, that their bark is worse than their bite.

In 1513 Machiavelli wrote his ageless treatise on leadership in the Italian politics of that day. He wrote about individual men and their way to power; what he said is important to us now because he saw with a fresh eye and described what he saw. And though the methods of the Borgias, Castruccios, and the Sforzas are not the methods of the followers of Penrose and Vare, yet in all probability the same motives that influenced the Italians have influenced the Philadelphia politicians. And I, though falling lamentably short of my peerless model, have always tried, in this study of a democratic urban society, to describe, first-hand, politicians and their tactics as I saw them to be, without advocating what I thought they ought to be.

Because I write about real men in politics, and flesh and blood voters, and give details and incidents for the most part as I have personally observed them to be,

INTRODUCTION

I think that whatever value this volume may possess will be permanent. Even if the Tony Nicollos, the George Kendalls, or the Nick Fishbournes should give way to other leaders because of a change in the *Zeitgeist*, or for any other reason, I believe that this description of politicians will still be valid as a cross-section of the party process, of the attitude and forces that motivate people in politics.

Both as a political scientist and as a citizen, I have always concentrated on trying to see the basic life forces in the governing process rather than the conventional forms—the man and his methods rather than the charters and constitutions. And I have found that, no matter what phase of the political process I was examining, I was repeatedly being brought back to the conditioning factor in that process, the politician himself.

He holds the center of the political stage in America; he is often both author and leading man of the political drama that everyone pays to see, whether he watches the play or not. And like an actor on the stage, the politician usually acts in a manner pleasing to that section of the audience that observes him closely. The greater public—those not interested in politics—often find that the politician is not seriously interested in them either, for he naturally puts his time and energy where it will count for the most; government will consider private and special interests rather than the common weal so long as only private-interest groups pay attention to what is happening on the boards.

But a convincing and unbiased picture of the politician I found very difficult to obtain. The persons who actually know politicians, for one reason or another, almost never write about them. As for the politicians themselves, they have other work to do, and other interests than writing. Or if by any chance they do write, they are going to write about their achievements—either an *apologia pro sua vita* or a tale of the bizarre among the band of brothers, not the natural, honest-to-goodness politician as he is in everyday life. Or if they do not write of the exceptional in their life, neither do they think of telling the details (so interesting to a student of politics) in connection with their march toward victory any more than a farmer would think of counting the number of potatoes in a bushel. The autobiography of William S. Vare, the boss, was published shortly before his death. One might read it entire without learning that officeholders are assessed by the party organization to help finance campaigns, or that all save one in a thousand in the organization in normal times obediently vote as directed without question.

With my dominant interest in the everyday life of the politician as my guide, I, as a fellow of the Social Science Research Council, undertook to make a first-hand study of him. I went to his native setting and lived with him there for fifteen months. To describe realistically the professional politician, I had to present him against his social, economic, and political background. His living portrait apart from the voters and the rest of the environment in his field of activity would be quite inadequate. It might be compared to a volume on hunting that minutely described the African lion and yet neglected to say that this animal is a monarch of

12

the jungles of Africa and is not found in his free state in other places. For the politician is, above all else, a child of his environment even though he is one of the factors that help fashion and maintain that environment.

So I went right to him, and it is with his knowing and unknowing cooperation that this book has been made possible. The men at City Hall knew me as the professor who was studying the politicians so that he could write a book about them as they actually were rather than as they are often imagined to be. With certain important exceptions I wrote the politician's words verbatim as we talked; to my satisfaction the speaker usually approved of this plan.

I attempt to present my findings here in a personal and informal way, in keeping with the manner of the men themselves. I present my characters as I found them. Those that are invariably profane in life are profane in my book; if the stuff of their language is rough, strong, and pungent in City Hall, so it is here; and those that speak with a degree of cultivation do so in these pages. Although I usually give the speaker a fictitious name, to hide his identity from the outer world, all else that I write is real. It is the politician himself speaking, as well as the political scientist.

Many important subjects relevant to the political process are not fully examined in this present volume even though they are of significance and interest. Here my main object has been to make a scientific study of the politician himself, from the inside looking out instead of from the outside looking in. Moreover, as I have said, I dwell on the normal and natural in the lives of these men rather than on the unique and spectacular, because I believe, with Justice Holmes, that "at this time we need education in the obvious more than an investigation of the obscure."

This volume is devoted to the division leader, not only because he is the political party's ambassador to the voter, the one that meets the citizen face to face, and carries the party leader's message to Garcia, but because he is the most indispensable factor in the organization and is himself an explanation for an overwhelming majority of political victories in our great urban centers. And even though he is only a ward politician, his influence merely begins in the neighborhood; ultimately it has a far wider scope, for in many elections at least one leg of the President's and governor's chairs (and in some cases, all four legs) rests squarely on the division leader's back.

I shall describe him in general terms and then follow the general with the particular in the form of a group of detailed sketches from life. The sketches are typical of widely different sorts of powerful leaders and have been selected from a great number of possible subjects. The defeat of the organization in 1933 is next described. And finally my book is concluded with a forecast as to new political attitudes, new governmental arrangements, and the "old regular" in the new politics.

>>->>-*>>-*>>-*>>-*>>*«*-«*-«*-«*-«*-«*

I
THE DIVISION
LEADER

●

THE PARTY'S AMBASSADOR
TO HIS MAJESTY
THE VOTER

>>->>-*>>-*>>-*>>-*>>*«*-«*-«*-«*-«*-«*

Service

>>>->>>->>>->>>->>>->>>->>>->>>->>>->>>->>>-<<<-<<<-<<<-<<<-<<<-<<<-<<<-<<<-<<<-<<<-<<<

I DO not know exactly how many fish there are in the sea, but we all know that the number is legion. I also imagine that not only the number of fish, but also the kinds and characteristics and colors of the creatures of the deep are myriad. However, in spite of the infinite variety, all have one function in common: *they survive because they can swim.* A similar statement can be made about politicians. There are preachers, gamblers, barbers, undertakers, high-school teachers, professors, elevator boys, university men, illiterates, gentlemen, and thugs in urban politics, but regardless of the diversity of the training, character, and ability of these individuals, they all have one function in common—*they serve their people.* And wherever one finds a powerful party organization in a great metropolitan center one will find that a large part of its strength is due to the personal service it renders its constituents—service which pricks the attention of the voter amid the buzzing confusion of life in a city. What the service is depends finally upon the wants of a people in a given area.

The party organization is strongest where the needs of the voters are most compelling. This explains why the most thoroughly controlled districts in either New

17

York, Chicago, Philadelphia, or any large city are nearly always likely to be those districts in which there is most unemployment, most conflict with the law, most difficulty in paying rent, buying food, and securing the other necessities of life; and these areas are more often than not districts in which a preponderant number of foreign-born or colored people live.

Fundamentally the work of the party organization revolves around these simplest fellow-creature wants: jobs—though the political party is more than an employment agency; food—although neither a political party nor a voter can live by bread alone; justice—tempered with mercy or favoritism; taxes—since the power to tax involves the power to destroy. The councilmen that levy the tax, the real-estate assessors, and the members of the board of revision of taxes are leaders in the party organization, not students of taxation. A friend at court in this field may be, and often is, worth dollars and cents to the voter—not only the small home owner, but the manufacturer and the utility operator as well.

The party is, basically, an intermediary between the citizen and the state. *Each according to his needs* is the service rule followed by the politician. For example, a Philadelphia manufacturer paid a $290,000 income tax under protest. Then the depression came and his business suffered; he tried to get the money refunded but could not. He appealed to the Boss. The leader thought that the case was a good one, and spoke to Mellon about it. The Secretary of the Treasury also considered the claim a good one and said that the money would be refunded in due course of time. The Boss said, "Hand it back now—this is urgent." Mellon did; and now this business

18

man and his family are for the organization, lock, stock, and barrel. And here is another example, of an entirely different sort. One night, at a ward club, an old-time ward leader and I talked for several hours. He recounted many of the favors that he had done for his constituents, but the one of which he was proudest concerned a young bride and her mother. This girl had been secretly married a few weeks before the first child was born. (At this point the leader explained that there is a saying in his ward that the first baby may be born any time but nine months are required for all other children.) The mother of the bride explained her sad plight to the ward leader. Something had to be done or the neighbors would talk. The leader had friends at City Hall, and he had the date on the marriage records moved back exactly one year. The mother was overjoyed; she explained that her daughter had secretly married a year before, and the modified diploma of marriage was framed and kept hanging on the wall for all to see. The daughter's life was not ruined. And she and her husband and the whole family always vote the ward leader's ticket.

These two services are spectacular rather than normal, but they suggest something of the range, or the length, of the politician's arm. I particularly do not want to convey the impression that what the division leader does for his voter is antisocial; it is sometimes that, as this book abundantly reveals, but more often it is an act of genuine social value. Philadelphia is a metropolis of 128 square miles and 2,000,000 people. The citizens elect 73 public officials from the city at large and 6,000 other officials in wards and districts in a cycle of four years—the citizen registering every year as well as voting once a year in a primary and election. The public servants who constitute the official government, are, for many citizens, part of the unseen environment of the great society in which they live. It is an environment that in normal times is often impersonal, remote, and meaningless to the people themselves until a wide-awake division leader appears before them in the flesh. He is an individual who speaks their own language and knows their wants. He often makes warm and personal that which had been cold and distant. He "knows everybody" at City Hall, or he knows someone who does. He bridges the gap between the unseen outer world and the inadequate citizen. About this service, Graham Wallas wrote, "It represents the most vigorous attempt which has been made to adapt the form of our political institutions to the actual facts of human nature."

I repeat that this "service motive" is not limited to ward politics, but goes all the way through our political life from the smallest office in the division to the most far-reaching in national or international affairs. The importance of the Rivers and Harbors Committee in Congress, for example, is an expression of the same principle as it applies to a group or constituency instead of a single person. Just as half a ton of coal or a discharge from a magistrate's court will swing the individual voter into line, so also can an entire constituency be captured by an appropriation for building a new post office or excavating a harbor or working on a canal. The Hennepin County Canal may never see a ship, but the man who got the appropriation for the County was none the less able to see Congress.

20

Even a cursory examination of the men at the Peace Conference at Versailles reveals that not one, with the possible exception of Woodrow Wilson, was concerned with the problems of the *common good*, the world problem, the canons of abstract justice, but that each of these delegates, whether it was Clémenceau of France, Lloyd George of England, Orlando of Italy, Saionji of Japan, or Paderewski of Poland, was thinking in terms of the advantages for his own national group. Each participant concerned himself almost exclusively with what he could do for his own state. Humanity as a whole had no spokesman, with the exception of President Wilson. And because Wilson centered his attention on the greater good and neglected factional interests at home, he was, although universally acclaimed, defeated on his return to the United States. Either the ward politician or the national leader might observe, "What does it profit a man to gain the approval of the whole world and lose that of his own bailiwick?"

The individual sketches of division leaders in a later section of this book will reveal in great detail the basic nature of this personal service to the voter. This chapter, however, will give a more general description of the division leader himself, his relation to the voter, and his place in the political process.

The Human Equation

In Philadelphia the point of contact between the electorate and the organization* is in the 1,283 divisions

* From about the turn of the century until 1932 there was only one party organization in Philadelphia; the Democratic end was part of the Republican

that comprise the fifty wards that are the city and county.† In each of these smallest electoral units there are two "sales agents" (ward committeemen or division leaders); usually one is "the" committeeman and the other is his lieutenant. Philadelphia, America's third city, follows the same technique in all of her elections, be the office at stake the Presidency or a division assessor-ship; and, as I have said, the most vital factor in twenty-nine out of thirty elections in normal times is the division leader—the personal sales agent of the party, who not only visits his sales territory, but lives in it. He meets

---

machine under another name. However, the impetus provided by the great depression, the weak leadership of the Republicans, and the New Deal program of the Federal government, dramatized by the brave and smiling face of Roosevelt and supplemented by his friendly voice over the radio and his attractive personality revealed in movies, has led to the creation of a new Democratic party—one that is free from Republican control. This newly created party, strengthened in 1933–1934 by Farley, Pinchot, and some local patronage (and now in 1935 it can look forward to more jobs from Senator Guffy and Governor Earle and newly elected Democratic Congressmen and state senators and assemblymen), is off to a good start. Furthermore, disgruntled Republican politicians have jumped on the Democratic band wagon. What this party's position will be in the future cannot be known at this time. According to all present evidence, however, any new party of significance will use the same technique that the Republicans use in winning elections—save that in the future the radio will play a more important part in campaigns than it has thus far in the United States. But the radio will be a supplement rather than a substitution for the technique herein described. The radio cannot explain a case to a magistrate, shake a man's hand, nor bring him a basket of groceries.

† All the committeemen in a ward form the ward committee. For example, if there are thirty divisions in a given ward there will be sixty members on the ward committee. Once a year the members of the ward committee elect a member to the city committee who is either the ward leader or the representative of the ward leader. The point of contact between the electorate and the party organization is in the 1,283 divisions. The ward committeeman is the liaison officer between the voters below and the ward leader above.

22

the voter face to face, and this is one important reason why the organization rarely loses in certain areas. (If it is good business for an old-line life-insurance company or a wholesale grocer to rely on salesmen in the field rather than on newspaper, magazine, radio, and mail advertising, how much more necessary is it for one who offers what is often remote and vague to have a representative personally call on the voter?)

The anti-organization candidate, unlike his opponent, invariably relies on a secondary—not a primary—appeal. In addition, his plea for a vote is likely to be centered around some nebulous or abstract idea like "more efficient administration" or "honest government." Intrinsically the realization of this ideal may hold more in store for the "man in the street" than does a smile from a friendly face, or a basket of groceries at Christmas time, but in the absence of catastrophes and depressions the majority of voters cannot be convinced of this merely through newspaper articles, editorials, talks over the radio, or political sermons given by strangers. And so they turn to the man who comes to them directly.

These division leaders—"ward heelers" in the patois of the independent—are the career men of politics in this country, the men who give all their time to this greatest of games. The most successful of them have no other interest, or, if they have other interests, they have no other gods. Politics and allied activities are their first thought. They are like soldiers in wartime—ready for service at any hour. As William S. Vare once described it to me, "The division leader must stay close to those who need him. He must be on the job to help them. The average division leader can always be found at a certain place—the corner cigar store, the drugstore, or some such place. He goes there every night. When the voter wants him he knows where to find him." Nor do the leaders limit themselves to the corner stores; often their homes are like clubs or offices. A dozen constituents may come in a group, or there may be a steady procession—a queue of faithful voters in trouble. Others may pay hurried calls on their leaders before breakfast. Day and night the telephone rings, for the leader or his family to answer. One leader's wife told me that it was a dog's life; but other wives, and the majority of them, really like it as well as their men do. They enjoy the feeling of power that comes to those that are indispensable in a community. Vare once told me the following incident and conversation:

"Seven years ago a division leader came to see me. His division was becoming filled with Russian Jews. His wife was dainty—she did not like to live or bring up her children in that sort of neighborhood. So this man came to my office and said that he was going to move. He asked me where would be a good place to go. I said, 'Move to West Philadelphia; everyone is new out there. The question of seniority cannot be raised against you out there.' After he had lived there he became leader of his division and was elected to his committee. This man was a third rater in South Philadelphia, but was first rate in West Philadelphia. Two years ago he came to see me. He said that he was going to quit being a committeeman—that he was not getting anything out of it. I said, 'In your division, how many people can

24

you call by their first names?' He said, 'About three hundred.' 'Now suppose you weren't in politics,' I said, 'how many would speak to you? About three! You have done something worthwhile with your life. How many nice women has your wife met?' He said, 'About thirty or sixty.' And I said, 'That is worth something to you.'"

The profession of politics as these men know it requires a lifetime of preparation. There are no short cuts, and there never were textbooks. The politician's college—the old corner saloon—has been either abolished or so completely emasculated that it no longer serves as the political forum where the beginner can learn from the lips of the master about the royal game of winning votes. The doctor or the engineer have single-faceted disciplines compared to the one imposed upon the followers of Vare and Penrose; and a textbook on politics seems as impossible to conceive of as one on love. In love, politics, and religion, there are intangible values that can never be put upon paper—to know them one must experience them first-hand. But there are a few very definite preliminary requisites for the politician. His first step in the preparation for his career is either to be born into a constituency made up of his own kind of people, or to move there as promptly as possible. The next step is to smile when he speaks to his neighbors—and he must speak to them. The last step is to the grave.

Motives

The individuals who devote their lives to politics are motivated differently, but an unusual number of them have an extraordinary socio-political awareness. This

25

fondness or sympathy for, or interest in, other people is not primarily a matter of reason; it may be due to the possession of a good digestive tract. The professional politician likes the "feel" of the life he follows. Or at least it is less distasteful than any other life that he knows. Other contributing factors that vary with individuals are centered in power, prestige, recognition, economic gain, the love of battle or contests, and the personal loyalty to some leader or to followers.

Start in Politics

When one asks the politicians how they got their start in politics there are many variations in detail in the answers, and yet the following statements illustrate the general tenor of 90 per cent of them. (This first one, however, is the only case I know of where political interest was manifest as early as the sixth year.)

"I remember going to the voting place and being asked if I wanted to vote. I stepped up to the window and said, 'Yes.' The window clerk wanted to know my name and age. I replied, 'Six years old.' When this man told me that I would have to wait fifteen years more I had tears in my eyes. 'What a long time to wait!' I thought. But it wasn't so long, for when I was eight I folded ballots. Ever since then I have been at the polls on election day, always looking on and listening to the politicians talk and often helping out. I am now fifty-eight years of age, and I have never lost my interest in campaigns and elections. I like to help the voters. I was elected to my ward committee when I was twenty-two, and I have never been off of it."

The next division leader speaks for many:

"I used to wait for election day as a kid waits for Christmas.

"I lived in the Second Ward. The democratic leader, George McGowan, asked me to help out at a primary election held for two hours in the evening. I was interested from the first. I was Democratic until George Vare started—then I became a Republican."

Many start in politics because someone did a valued favor for them. An answer like this is common:

"I ran away and got married when I was twenty-one. She was a Jew and eighteen. When we came back her father wanted to have me arrested. He sent a detective to my home. A politician lived across the street. My sister went to him; he called the detective off and told him not to bother me. Two days later he asked me to help him out at the polls. I did, and have been active ever since. First I was a watcher, then a clerk, then on the registration board, and next judge of elections."

One of the better educated negroes spoke for a large minority group of committeemen generally in making the following statement. His pessimistic note at the end is real—a sign of the present discontents in Philadelphia:

"I was around twenty when I first got interested in politics. I voted on age. I worked to get people to the polls right at the start. Sometimes it is interesting, and sometimes not. I had a liking for being with people and helping them. I went on the ward committee when I was thirty-two. I never had any desire for it before that. The older men couldn't have stopped me; I had the men in I wanted. When the right man comes along now I'll let him be ward committeeman; I don't want it. I am tired of it. There is lots of things about it a person wouldn't like—things that a person should do but can't—you can't give the proper help because the help ain't there. You can't get no jobs. You can't help them financially because you ain't got enough yourself. If you are in it you are in it to help yourself and you can't help others."

Failing health of a certain sort is another major reason for going into politics:

"I was an electrician and my kidneys were bad. The doctor told me that I could not stand heavy work. I had lots of friends, ran for the committee, got a job here at the Hall; that was seventeen years ago. I will never leave—I like the life."

The next statements explain the presence of many of the university men on party committees:

"I got interested in politics in 1915. A candidate for office promised me a fellowship if he got elected. He didn't get elected, and I did not get my fellowship, but I made enemies. These political enemies made it unpleasant for me and I worked against them. In 1920 I got elected to the ward committee largely because of this experience. A member of council was a friend of mine; he had done me a favor. His partner on the committee was jealous and sore. He was against me, so I displaced him. I did it in three elections and have been on the committee ever since."

Entering politics because of a desire for revenge or a feeling of hate is a fairly common reason; indifference of the following sort toward a job, however, is not:

28

"Voting was a religion in my family. I went to vote one night about two minutes past seven o'clock. The committeeman wouldn't let me vote. This infuriated me, and I told him that he would never have a chance to keep anyone else away from voting. Next year I was a candidate against him and won. I was a committeeman for eleven years before I got a job. I did not want one. I am in politics because I like it." (Now he has a job in City Hall, however.)

Jobs

The occupations of the party committeemen, like their personal characteristics, are nearly as varied as those listed in the city directory; in reality, "the little fellow in politics" is likely to have his name in every directory save one—the social register. (But even if his own name is not there, nor his ward leader's either, yet he may be represented in it by the man that is responsible for his ward leader.) Each one of the fifty committees in Philadelphia contains one or more attorneys among its members or close friends. In a river ward there will be one, two, or three lawyers on the committee, or near it—perhaps 2 to 5 per cent of its membership; in such independent wards as the Twenty-second, Forty-second, or Forty-sixth, the percentage of lawyers on the committee is greater—10 to 15 per cent on the committee may be lawyers. Other committeemen are barbers, storekeepers, salesmen, advertising men, plumbers, laundrymen, school teachers, gamblers, musicians, bootleggers, doctors, undertakers, chiropractors, dentists— and I know one veterinary surgeon; but horses are few,

29

and he gives all of his working hours to caring for "the wants of his people"—the division leader's definition of politics.

Of course, whether or not they have a profession, trade, or outside job, about 85 per cent of the committee-men in the most strongly organized Philadelphia wards (for example, those eighteen wards that Vare carried in November, 1933) are on the public pay roll; and in the semi-organization and independent wards about 40 to 65 per cent are there.* The number of party workers and leaders with jobs at City Hall is decidedly greater than these percentages indicate. They refer only to party workers that have been elected to the ward committee, whereas in a number of divisions the most powerful politician is not on the ward committee, but he is on the City Hall pay roll. (The Philadelphia charter forbids jobholders to engage in politics; however that does not always prevent their doing it.) There is no similar restriction against county employees' serving on party committees and being active in politics. The organization's finest are in county departments in City Hall, though many of these are holding places under the charter.

Ed Vare once said, "Take care of your people and your people will take care of you." This is true, with exceptions, today. A producer, a live-wire committeeman that carries his division in every election, is bound to get a job, because he has something that the organization

---

* I am grateful to Mr. D. H. Kurtzman of Philadelphia for permitting me to see two tables that he prepared on the number of ward committeemen on the public pay roll in 1931, and the salaries that they received.

needs—votes. A governor is in the offing with state patronage, and it behooves the organization to select its place holders with discernment. The lowliest party worker knows that a block of votes is legal tender at City Hall, and a leader's incentive for continually nursing along his constituency is never lacking. It therefore follows that there is apt to be a strain of almost sentimental hopefulness in the politician's make-up. And although jobs are fewer in 1933 and 1934 than they were in 1932 or earlier, yet the optimistic "little fellows" continually ask their harassed ward leaders, "How long, oh Lord, must I wait before I too am recognized with an appointment!"

In politics it is assumed that a man is trained for any place in the public service he can get. This explains the variety of public positions held by committeemen. Four are members of the state senate, twenty-six of the legislature, four of Congress; nineteen are magistrates; twenty are councilmen (including ten that are also members of the city committee); others hold positions in the courts, in the bureau of weights and measures, and in such offices as those of the coroner, the district attorney, the mercantile appraiser, the prothonotary, the recorder of deeds, the register of wills, the revision of taxes, the real-estate assessors, the sheriff, and the controller.

The job that is the cynosure of many eyes in Philadelphia is that of tipstave; it pays $3,000 a year; like appointment to the Federal supreme court, it is for life, and standing guard for the "honorables" is not onerous. But the average salary connected with these jobs is about $1,800 a year; some places pay more, some less.

However, there are sometimes opportunities for earning extra money on the side. A tenement-house inspector at $1,800 said that he would not trade his place for a $5,000-a-year job; he was getting more than that out of it. Another inspector, in the weights and measures bureau, is content to remain there at $1,800 although he could get another position at $2,800. Those who are so fortunate as to be secretaries to magistrates usually value their places more highly than the official salaries would lead one to expect.

There are more ways, however, of deriving financial benefit from one's activity in politics than by merely being connected with the public pay roll. For example, in the M Ward, all the ward committeemen except three have jobs in City Hall. One of these three I shall call Snake Gleason; he has a part interest in a brick company, and, through the influence and help of his ward leader, he has sold the city and the school board many bricks. The second, Mr. M., owns a cigar store, and manages it as well; he has been a committeeman for more than thirty years, and has not asked for a job. Recently, however, his son was given a pleasant position in the City Hall annex, at $5,000 a year. The third, Henry Bottom, is an attorney; I quote his words as to what politics means to him. "I have received eight masterships [a mastership pays $100 for a few hours' work in a divorce proceedings] since the first of the year, but I have had only one from Augie [the ward leader]. I got the rest through judges that I know myself. I do not want Augie's masterships. I am making between $4,000 and $5,000 a year, and I can stand on my own feet. The

32

organization is not feeding me; besides, when I have a case with a $1,000 fee, I want to be able to go to Augie and say, 'See here, I want you to speak to this judge for me,' and Augie will do that, and I will be able to put my man on probation. You see, this is worth a lot more to me than a $100. Not long ago Augie asked me if I wanted a couple of masterships. I said, 'No, there are too many lawyers who need it that are on your neck—give it to them.' He said, 'That is very nice of you, Henry.'"

In addition to masterships there are a number of other sinecures for the most successful of the legally trained committeemen, such as auditorships and receiverships. And some committeemen, as I have said, hold elective positions ranging from judge and Congressman to magistrate, councilman, assemblyman, constable, school visitor, and assessor. When the division leader is advanced to the bench, however, he usually resigns from his ward committee.

The division leader's job depends invariably upon one or two factors—either his productivity as a party worker, or, less often, his friendship for some prince of the party. Just as jobs in the public service are sometimes given without regard to the public, so may jobs in the party's control be given without any careful regard for the organization. Here a merit system of a kind is followed more often than in public service, but even here nepotism and personal friendship count. This weakens the morale of any service. In August, 1933, I was eating luncheon in a Horn and Hardart restaurant with an active and ambitious party worker who has a minor position at City Hall. He abruptly pointed to a man in a gray suit that was eating at a near-by table. "See that fellow. His name is ——. His father was an old Vare man for thirty years, and now he is on a pension. Just recently Vare had the son made a court clerk at $5,000 a year. The same thing happened with ——, etc. That's what hurts."

Love of the Game

The lure of the approaching presidential campaign in 1912 caused T. R. the First to abandon lion hunting in Africa and come home. When politics gets into a man's blood, he stays in it without any reasoned hope of reward, just as other men go on playing cards, drinking liquor, betting on the horse races, or hunting quail and mallard. Something of this feeling for the sport element in politics is inherent in more than 90 per cent of the politicians.

The regular in politics, like the professional military man, loves the life. He may be working for his pocketbook even as a merchant is working for his, but there is more to it than that. Though he must have a job, even as the rest of us must, he often prefers a $25 job in City Hall to a $50 job in industry. The life there is full of the unexpected and the uncertain—elements lacking in many trades and professions. Furthermore, the lack of a formal education may not be the handicap in politics that it is in other fields. It is unfortunate that Horatio Alger missed this great field and theme. Civic affairs might have been invested with a glamour which they do not now possess in the general mind, for the

34

truth is there are far more men that were originally rail-splitters holding high public office than are to be found in the seats of the mighty in the world of high finance.

And the professional politician woos the fickle public more as a man engaged than married, for his is a contract that must be renewed every two years, and the memory of the public is short. He thrives on the "warm embrace" of the crowd, and cannot afford to be far from it and all the planning, plotting, and incessant talking that goes with the life. After my sketch of Tony Nicollo had appeared in the *Yale Review*, a committeeman from the Thirty-fourth Ward wrote, "You certainly hit the nail on the head in the last line of the article—'No king ever surveyed his realm with greater satisfaction.' When I go home at night and even the little children say, 'Good evening, Mr. Johnson,' it makes me feel very good." The wish in men's lives for recognition may be as real as the desire for wealth, and a combination of the two, such as politics often is, can create an urge that will carry men far.

Characteristics

The division leaders have varying characteristics, just as the people in different sections of Philadelphia have different traditions, different ethical and moral codes, different racial and nationality patterns, economic standards, cultural attitudes, and mental habits. For the real politician is a natural phenomenon, not a legal device; and he is a prototype of his people, not a "sport" or a freak. If he were not "of the people" and interested (for one reason or other) in their personal problems, he could not survive. However in spite of great variety of personality types in politics,* the professional, as I have said before, is more likely to be the spiritual kin of Aaron Burr than of the unbending John Quincy Adams. He has Cavalier rather than Puritan blood in his veins. He holds, with Bentham, that the punishment should fit the person, not the crime.

Loyalty

The most striking single identifying quality of these division leaders (and the majority of the ward leaders, too), who have consciously or unconsciously chosen politics as a career, is loyalty. These men are loyal to their leaders just as their leaders are in turn loyal to their own leaders and the organization. It is personal rather than civic loyalty. This loyalty pattern is a habit of mind among the overwhelming majority of the members of any successful party organization. It is so implicit in normal times that one must turn, in nature, to a highly trained bird dog to find its counterpart, or to a young child's faith in its parent. In a free moment, these men unhesitatingly describe themselves as "order

* There are also women among the party organization workers, and in 1932 seven were elected to the ward committee—four in a river ward, one in an old Penrose ward, and two in the independent Germantown sector. However, as in the case of certain men, one of these women is on the committee in name only. Her brother, a rather old man and the occupant of a position under the city charter, is the real committeeman. He makes a perfunctory gesture toward the charter provision that denies a municipal employee the privilege of engaging in politics; he engages in politics just the same, but under his sister's name. I might add that this small group of women reflect the constituencies which they represent exactly as the greater number of male committeemen do.

men." They take orders and ask no questions (and neither do they answer any unless they are told to). One of the Hon. Dick Weglein's men in the Twenty-ninth Ward told me he would go to hell if Sheriff Weglein told him to, for he knew that Weglein would not tell him to go to hell unless he had some good reason. The sheriff, in turn, was a follower and friend of the late Tom Cunningham, and, in the summer of 1931, when Cunningham told Weglein that he was not the Republican party's candidate for mayor, the loyal leader of the Twenty-ninth was painfully disappointed, but thought no more of the matter. He is now sheriff, and there is to be another mayoralty election in 1935.

Mr. Fred Lunt, who is now leader of the XYZ Ward and president of the —— ——, is so much an order man that a prominent Philadelphia newspaper man recently remarked, "If Senator Vare were to tell Fred Lunt to set fire to Independence Hall, he would do it!" Or, to put it in Freddie Lunt's own words: "My platform is short, sweet, and easy to say—I am for William S. Vare."

Jim Mulvihill is chairman of the —— Ward committee and has been a division leader for seventeen years. Not long ago he was a candidate for magistrate. The leaders of the organization slated someone else for the place. Primary election came and Jim not only worked against himself among the voters in his division, but voted for his favored opponent, and so did his wife. They are order men. As Bob Heinze, one of the most picturesque of them, once said, "When you are in Rome, you can't give the pope orders. You got to take orders."

One time I asked a question of the late Mr. Harry Freeston. He was one of the more intelligent division leaders, a fine old gentleman, then in his seventies, slender and ascetic in appearance, one who had been successfully active in division and ward politics for more than fifty years. I inquired whether he ever wished for a free vote—the same sort of vote that, theoretically at least, every citizen has. "You are part of the organization—you always vote the way you are told. There must be times when you want to vote according to your personal preference. You can't always agree with the slate-makers. Isn't there such a thing as loyalty to your own opinion as well as loyalty to your ward leader? How would you answer this question?"

Mr. Freeston had politely waited for me to finish, and then he promptly said, "Professor, that question has never come up."

I later received from other division and ward leaders this same reply when I put this question concerning the effect on the spirit of "order-voting." There are exceptions, but to the great majority of the organization men, although there are many questions that do confront them, this question is not one of them. I suppose that the organization politician's attitude is similar to that of the trained expert in the legislative reference library—one who drafts measures that members of the legislature bring to him, but whose entire thought and energy are concentrated on the mechanics of bill drafting, not on the social purpose of the measure. The party committee-men are concerned just as exclusively with the mechanics of politics, but not politics in the larger aspects, for

38

to them there is no politics in politics. They are order men, and, although their materials are human beings, the more these human beings act like automatons, the happier is their political shepherd.

One of the two very rare exceptions to the loyalty rule within recent times—occasions when certain organization men wanted to vote for the party's opponent, not its candidate—occurred in 1928. Men who normally say, "My motto is: what the ward leader is for, I am for," (and the ward leader in turn thinks, "What Vare is for, I am for; if he sinks, I sink with him")— these men are likely to say about the 1928 contest, "Let me tell you, a lot of the committeemen were heart and soul for Al Smith. He was one of the boys. I was in Tom Carrow's division. In order to see that we voted right I walked in with him and he walked in with me as we voted."

But even in a jolt like this one, and in so unusual a situation, the organization man saw to it that there were no derelictions in his own family. One leader, ten years out of law school, told me the following story: "Usually my wife, for instance, votes the way I tell her to vote— or rather, I go in and vote for her. All married people go in together and that is considered perfectly all right; married people can go in without having the judge of elections or anyone else ask them any questions. However, my wife is a college woman, and in this particular election she was very much interested in Al Smith. She said, 'Harry, grant me a favor this time; let me vote alone at this election.' I didn't say anything. When election day came I was standing in the polling place.

When the election officers started to hand her a ballot, I took it and walked in with her. I marked a straight Republican ticket and went out and put it in the ballot box before she could say anything.''

The other exception—that of 1933 and 1934—is different in kind. Many party workers, because of the depression, have been removed since 1931 from the public pay roll, and others are seeing less chance of getting on, in times like these. The general dissatisfaction of both politicians and public has broken traditions that in a prosperous era would have remained impregnable. A party worker without a job or, what is more important, without hope of a job, is apt to be uncertain in his loyalties. This may suggest that the identifying characteristic of the party worker's loyalty is that it is *a loyalty to winners.* *

* The bedrock basis of this loyalty pattern is security or the probability of security. In 90 per cent of the elections in Philadelphia the Republican party is paramount; its ward leaders are supreme in their domains, fixed and stationary in the political arrangements that all but encompass the lesser lieutenants in the party ranks. These ward leaders can usually give political advancement or take it away. Therefore, the division leader is loyal to his ward boss because in that unswerving loyalty lies his hope of future reward. Furthermore, there is no satisfactory alternative; rival leaders lack the credentials of the recognized ward leader; the people are unreliable and uncertain. But the situation changed during the third year of the great depression, and after. Now there is a rival party with its appealing leader in the White House, its governor at the state capitol, its register of wills and coroner in City Hall; the jobs—jobs—jobs are going to the Democrats. And what is more serious the Democratic party's leader presents an appeal so vivid that it was as if President Roosevelt had been present at every polling place on Tuesday (election day) according to a *New York Times* editorial. So colossal a foeman bewilders the Republicans; they do not know how to answer him, though Senator Huey P. Long may help. However, so long as there is a popular Democracy in the offing, and the Republican ticket is difficult to sell at home, loyalty will be put to its severest test. Some

40

Race—Religion

Another most frequent characteristic of committeemen is that they usually have the same race, and nationality origins, and religious beliefs as the dominant groups in the given area which they represent. In a negro division, one of or both the organization leaders are apt to be colored. The Italian, Irish, Jewish, and Slavic sections choose men of their own sort; so do the highly cultured, well-born communities, on the one hand, and the industrial and slum districts on the other. Those who cannot speak English at all, or who can speak it only a little, naturally choose one who is articulate in their native tongue as well as in English. I have been, for example, at the homes of foreign-speaking division leaders and have heard no word of English spoken except to me, for hours at a stretch. The foreign-born voter tells his troubles to his countryman in his native tongue, for he knows no other. His countryman helps him in the name of the Republican party; its platform may be meaningless, its ballot incomprehensible, but its division leaders render personal service that counts. The inevitable result of the functioning of the democratic process is that the type of man elected is descriptive of the general run of his constituents.

Energy

And there is one other especially outstanding necessity for the man who goes into politics—and that is that he

leaders go over to the Democratic side as forty years ago, and earlier, Democratic leaders renounced their party and joined the Republicans; other leaders are uncertain.

possess a superabundance of physical energy of the sort that can keep steadily renewing itself. The life-long politician often wins elections merely because of this indefatigable energy; his success is dependent far more on legwork than on brainwork. His life is one where lungs, liver, a strong stomach, and a tough skin are primary requisites. When Charlie Seger, the leader of the Seventh Ward, and before that, a committeeman, died in 1919, the *Public Ledger* published a statement that to a varying extent is true of all regulars in politics: "The main lesson to be obtained from the passing of Charles Seger is that if you give up twenty-four hours of a day to politics, you can succeed at it." When I asked the present ward leaders, who once had been division leaders, how much time they gave to politics, one said, "Never out of it!" Another answered, "It's like a fireman running to a fire." One of the most prominent ones explained: "To be successful in politics you mustn't count the hours; you go into the day and into the night." And I have spent enough time in City Hall and at the homes of the politicians to know that these answers are more realistically descriptive than lyrical.

An organization politician is often forced to surrender not only his own free time, but his family's too. Frank Simone has been a committeeman for many years; he is now advanced in age and has been working at City Hall in the heart of the day, and among his people in the morning and at night. The life is not an easy one. He commented, "My wife has been at the hospital and I brought her home last night. She said, 'Frank, I'm afraid to go home.' 'Why?' I said. 'The interruptions—

42

the people ringing the telephone at all hours of the day and night. I don't get a moment's rest and peace.' Now it is worse because of the unemployment crisis. There are 350 voters in my division; suppose each one wanted a job, what could I do? I am called upon a lot; at the dinner table, in bed, at any hour.''

Mr. Simone looked very tired when he talked, but he had no thought of giving up. ''I know nothing else to do,'' he said. About a month ago I read an obscure notice in the *Philadelphia Record:* ''City Hall Worker Dies,'' and learned that Mr. Simone's life of service had ended.

Once while talking to a committeeman in his law offices we were interrupted by his young wife who had been following our conversation. I shall call her Mrs. Blake. She is the clinging-vine type of wife and she expressed great discouragement over her marriage because ''Politics takes all of Tom's time. He seems to prefer loafing on street corners and going out with the boys to staying home with me. I know that he wouldn't be anything if he didn't go out and meet people and talk to them. He wants the people to know who he is when he comes around before election to ask them for their vote.

''Just the same, this is awfully hard on me. He is not at home very much and when he is, so many people come to see him, asking favors of one sort or another. There is no social life at all—it's all politics. He doesn't steal votes,'' Mrs. Blake added, ''but I think it would be all right if he did because he does so much for the people.''

43

Probably all that can be said on the subject may be summed up in a short story that Colonel Dillon tells about Joe Nobre (for a generation leader of the Second Ward), and a drunken constituent who asked Nobre to give him some money.

"As old-timers do not need to be told, Nobre made his office in the kitchen of his home. He had a big roll-top desk in one corner of the roomy kitchen and here he sat, on designated evenings, to receive his division men and such other callers as had business with him. One evening while I was sitting there with Joe, a stuttering person wanted Nobre to lend him two dollars.

"Why should I lend you two dollars?" asked Nobre. "You're no use politically."

"I-is th-that s-so!" said the stuttering individual. "W-well l-let m-me t-tell y-you s-something y-you d-don't kn-know. I-I c-can c-carry the s-sixth d-division a-any t-time I w-want t-to."

"You can?" said Nobre. "Well, why don't you?"

"D-do y-you w-want t-to kn-know w-why?" asked McCandless.

"I do." said Nobre. "Tell me why."

"B-because," said the stuttering individual, "it's t-too d-damn m-much t-trouble!"

"Here's the two dollars," said Nobre. "There's a lot of people who don't carry them for that same reason, but they're not quite as frank as you are."

In addition to loyalty, common race and religion, and superabundant energy, the most powerful ward politicians know their people and know how to get

44

along with them, are resourceful, and keep their eyes on the next step, untroubled by any ideal of a distant and abstract good.

Fraud

The presence, absence, or, more pertinently, the extent of fraud in politics is necessarily conditioned by the attitude of the people toward fraud generally, and the efficacy of the safeguards devised to prevent it. It is a problem of education as well as of mechanics of control. Our education has been faulty in that our emphasis is invariably on *winning* rather than on *fair play* or *sportsmanship*. In business or in football the most vital questions are posited on how much money was accumulated, how many games were won. Public attitudes powerfully influence private actions. Penal statutes also influence them. In the majority of wards of Philadelphia both methods of social control are found to a varying degree, and here fraudulent political tactics are correspondingly reduced. In other parts of the city the only effective check against fraud is the criminal law. However this law requires men to enforce it; and in times of prosperity and when there is no strong contest against the organization, the law is measurably less effective than in "wartime," as in 1933–1935, when the opposition is vigilant and at the polls. However the presence of fraud in politics can easily be overemphasized; the great majority of politicians who succeed over a period of years have something positive to offer their people. They cannot build a career on fraud alone.

45

Strong-arm Methods

The politicians would hold, with Machiavelli, that it is much "safer to be feared than loved when, of the two, either must be dispensed with; for love is preserved by the link of obligation which, owing to the baseness of men, is broken at every opportunity for their advantage; but fear preserves you by a dread of punishment that never fails." And there are times, in some close election fights and in a certain type of neighborhood, when the iron fist is used in case the subtler service argument fails. Here, for a time, there are no rules, and might prevails—and might is invariably on the side of the organization and the division leader, for the organization is part of the government, and the government hires the police. The following illustrations may stand for many.

"During the Smith-Hoover contest, a staunch Catholic was the watcher for the opposition. He refused money, he refused a job. He hung on. Sam McCool, a fellow Catholic, working for Hoover, couldn't budge him. All of a sudden, after McCool left, I [the organization committeeman] looked up and saw the watcher and a stranger [non-resident] rolling on the floor, pummelling each other. I shoved them out into the street where, it so happened, two plain-clothes men hustled them to the hoosegow. The watcher was released at 11 P.M., the young stranger in an hour. Incidentally, Magistrate Blank, a former pugilist, got his start in the ABC Ward that way."

Another strong-arm leader explained his method in winning over watchers when a fight would be inex-

46

pedient. "Two very persistent Jews appeared as Roosevelt watchers in the last election. I gave them both the price of a breakfast and made them dissatisfied with the $2.00 they were getting from the Roosevelt group. I hinted that the leader was holding out on them. Next I paid each $10—and promised them a job I didn't have; this got them outside for the rest of the day." This same leader was arrested later that day. The charge was giving a negro fifty cents and pushing him out of the polling place. George, the leader, admits both charges, but says that the negro was drunk and was demanding more money; to grant that would have been a bad precedent. "The next day the colored man was offered some liquor by one of the 'boys' in the neighborhood. Then some of my friends taunted him. When he started to fight, the policeman on the beat clubbed him to a pulp, and took him to the hospital for repairs—he was badly damaged. Next, Magistrate Timbull sent him up for three months. He never returned to the division, and the charge was dropped."

Force is sometimes used with storekeepers and small business concerns, too, when they cannot be won over by favors. Perhaps the dealers will be interested in an anti-organization candidate who is campaigning on a popular issue. The police, cooperating with the committeeman, may perhaps use some such method as the following to bring them around. The leader will select two or three business men in each block and have them summoned before the magistrate for some infraction of the law. The magistrate lectures the victims, but adds that they have a good friend in their ward committee-

47

man—"else it would go hard with you!" If the store-keepers are fined, the committeeman personally returns the fine. The next time they vote, they usually go along with the organization ticket.

A prominent division leader told me how he once used the majesty of the law to please some of his people. Some of his voters came to him complaining that colored people had moved next door to them. The leader promised to do what he could for them and immediately set to work to please the people in his division. He first went to the home of the colored people and asked them to kindly move out. They naturally resented this, and refused to move. Then the division leader resorted to other means. He went to City Hall and reported his case to a city employee. In a few days an inspector for the bureau of health called at the home of the colored people. He showed his credentials and was permitted to inspect the house. After going through the house he told the people that a number of improvements would have to be made on the property because it was in an unsanitary condition. The improvements he suggested would cost several thousand dollars. But this was not all—for later in the day a representative from the electrical bureau called to examine the house wires. After inspecting the house he too told the colored folks that such and such would have to be done. The colored people now began to realize that they could not outdo the division leader, and within a week's time they vacated the premises. The division leader told me that he had not yet finished with these people when they left, for,

48

had they remained, the assessments on the property would have been raised, and other hardships would have been inflicted upon them. It was not his will to be harsh with the colored family, but he had to take care of his voters before the next election.*

Bribery

Force of the sorts that I have just described gives the political worker a certain sense of security, even though it be a false one, and even though it is effective, with few divisions excepted, only in peace times, when the opposition is weak. There is also another device of the same sort, used by the ineffective committeeman who fails to serve his people and has to resort to drastic means for keeping his control—and that is the purchase of votes. There are various kinds of vote-buying, of course, direct and indirect, and both are resorted to in certain neighborhoods. When it comes to buying votes, a subtler method than buying them outright (one that is often used to win support which is impervious to smiles and argument) is to hire the indifferent or hostile individual as a party worker. This may mean that an organization candidate may have forty or even one hundred workers in certain divisions in a hot fight—each to receive not less than $5.00 or $10.00 for the day. His first service is to vote for his employer and if he can help out in some other way, so much the better. I know an apartment

* See my "An Election Episode" in the *National Municipal Review*, October, 1934.

house in which nineteen voters live. One of the nineteen sometimes receives $50 for the vote of the house. He divides with the rest. Theoretically he is paid $50 to work for the ticket.

A prop provided by law for the purchase of votes is the "assistance to voters" clause that enables the voter to have assistance in marking his ballot in case he cannot read the names on the ballot unaided. This provision is often most liberally interpreted (see page 149), and the organization worker walks into the polling booth with a voter that is obligated to the leader.

Another provision of the law (abolished in 1933) that fostered a form of bribery was one requiring the payment of a tax (a poll tax of 25 cents) as a prerequisite to voting. The organization in the past provided the faithful with these receipts. When Ed Vare died, Dave Lane, "the peerless leader," said, "Mr. Vare was good to the poor—he bought tax receipts for them so they could vote." A voter entering the polling place used to be asked to show his receipt. He had none. One might be given to him; he put down a coin, and was told to keep it. Another might have asked for a receipt and neglected to pay for it; the oversight would be called to his attention. Whether the voter paid for his tax receipt or not in some wards depended on who the voter was.

However, the strength of the organization in the fifty wards generally is a positive thing, based, as I have said, on service to voters. Bribery, ballot-box stuffing, padded registration lists exist in selected areas. These and other fraudulent practices swell the total vote that the

50

party receives, but the organization, in times of tension, survives if it survives at all without these aids.

Values

The quality of one's interest in the ballot depends on what the vote symbolizes. To the politician it may represent a job, personal prestige, or possibly victory in the most crucial battle of the year or of a life. Its value in this case is tangible, concrete, and of the here and now. It stands for something seen and felt. Also it may appear as a reward or the pay-off for services performed. A person with a private end in view is likely to feel an interest in the ballot foreign to the purpose of the individual who is thinking merely in terms of the common good.

To the citizen that is not a politician the ballot is likely to symbolize a more intangible ideal, a more remote program of official action. The vote's significance is here indirect and more of the future than of the present. What the ballot actually means will depend on the political education of the citizen generally, and the extent to which issues and the personalities of candidates come within the range of the electorate's active attention. A candidate who can present politics as theater, dramatize issues as did Al Smith in 1928, or as did Roosevelt in 1934, or make a face-to-face appeal for support will enhance the voter's interest in his ballot. At other elections however, the issues, the candidates, and the total electoral process may be so meaningless that less than half the potential electorate will concern themselves enough about the ballot to mark it.

51

Politician's Attitude toward the Vote

The remark of Mrs. Blake, in commenting on her husband's incessant activity in politics, "He doesn't steal votes, but I think it would be all right if he did, because he does so much for the people," is most revealing, for it gives the authentic attitude of ward committeemen toward votes—their votes; according to the politician's catechism, "If I serve a man, his vote is morally mine" or "I work 365 days a year for him, he works one day for me—that's all I ask."

It is for such reasons as these that the attitude of organization men toward the sacred ballot will always be poles apart from what is written concerning it in newspapers and books, or from the views held by independents and reformers.* To the former groups, the vote is a commodity that has been bought and paid for many times (service for votes); and to the latter group

* For an example of this other attitude toward the ballot, note the following: "And what means universal suffrage? That every person of sound mind and of the age which common custom fixes as the time test of responsibility, shall freely, fully, potently express his ideas for his own, and for the general welfare. To enfranchise man is to give liberty to the mind, and to let the world have the benefit of ideas. Nations rest upon men; men upon ideas. The franchise is a political device by which ideas may be known, counted, weighed and applied. In the evolution of government, we are now [1897] in the franchise process. The device is practicable, and when fairly used, serves a large purpose in American democracy. But on the last analysis, it is only a device. The real struggle for the franchise is not to win a piece of political mechanism, but to win freedom of thought, political morality—the republic of ideas. The device itself is the political compliment which in the evolution of democracy is paid to the thoughtless. The apology for the device is that its extension tends to make men and women thoughtful." (Francis N. Thorpe, "A Century's Struggle for the Franchise in America," *Harper's Magazine*, January, 1897.)

52

it is a privilege to be carefully exercised according to the dictates of one's own conscience and intellect. To give it for any other reason is to prove unworthy of this high prerogative. Just as the police power of the state should not be bartered away, neither should the individual's franchise. But the effect of one vote is so small, the social end in view is so vague and distant that for many people it belongs to their neighborhood committeeman. To them the contest most often is one between their Nick Fishbournes and Tony Nicollos versus X (the unknown). Nick and Tony are the men that domesticate the universal. The general action of the official government is, like the atmosphere, difficult for the people to see. The voter wants something personal and concrete, here and now. "Ward politics is an amplified scheme of family communism, a modernized clan," according to Robert A. Woods. The Nicks and Tonys are a kind of chieftain, and in many divisions the moral implication of their leadership is not even considered. The strongest division leaders that I have closely observed unknowingly agree—and this suggests that their people agree—with Jack Falstaff's statement in *Henry IV* concerning honour:

Well, 'tis no matter; honour pricks me on. Yea, but how if honour pricks me off when I come on? How then? Can honour set to a leg? no: or an arm? no. . . . What is honour? a word. What is in that word honour? what is that honour? air. A trim reckoning! Who hath it? he that died o' Wednesday. Doth he feel it? no. . . . 'Tis insensible, then? yea, to the dead. But it will not live with the living? no. Why? detraction will not suffer it. Therefore I'll none of it. Honour is a mere scutcheon; and so ends my catechism.

53

Many citizens, in Philadelphia and elsewhere, indignantly reject Falstaffian reasoning of this sort, and actually vote—when they do vote—according to their best judgment. But this group's influence is measurably less than it might be, partly because these more thoughtful citizens may not vote at all, or vote only on rare occasions. And they are more likely to vote in the final elections than in the primaries. Even when the tide was running strongly against the organization in 1933, the organization was nevertheless able to determine the Republican nominees for that year, though this time it failed in controlling the nominations of the Democratic party. Again, with the exception of a year like 1933, these more thoughtful voters are most likely to vote for Republican nominees (Philadelphia is the Gibraltar of Republicanism). There is also a residence handicap that prevents an undue proportion of Philadelphia's finest citizenry from voting for city officials—so many outstanding individuals live in the suburbs. Finally, these more conscientious voters are rarely organized, one opinion is as good as another, and their strength is scattered and thereby materially weakened.

Public Opinion

One may ask, "What of public opinion?" What indeed. The live-wire committeemen—the ones that always carry their division—hold their leaderships because they have no opinions on public questions, or they have no freedom of opinion concerning current civic problems. To think and to hold opinions, as posited by democratic theory, would lead to friction and destroy the oligarchy.

They have given a lifetime of labor to the building of their leadership; they have the artist's love of his work, the capitalist's interest in his investments. Risk all this for a free expression of opinion? Never. And their people would not think of asking that of them.

It is true that there are important exceptions where the division leader does not serve the people and may be unusually well informed on the political topics of the day; instead of telling the citizens how he wants them to vote, he may modestly state the facts as he sees them, and then allow the sovereign citizen to decide how he will mark his ballot. T. Henry Walnut is a committeeman of this sort in Philadelphia; he is outstanding in character, intellect, and interest; he adorns any society in which he lives. But men of this sort are not common in any group, and those that are on ward committees, even for a two-year term, are, like the musk ox of the north, very rare. The strength and nature of the organization are not fashioned out of such materials. These divisions go the way they list, and they are as likely to be against the organization ticket as for it.

As for the powerful division leader's part in the formulation of public opinion, it is similar to the action of neutralizers in chemistry, or of insulators in electricity. He is himself a neutralizer; he does not contribute in any way to a rational discussion of public questions, or help make a social judgment, even in these bitter days of depression. He, like Lippmann's Congressman, never thinks of dissipating his energy on public affairs; he prefers to do "a little service for a lot of people on a lot of little subjects, rather than to engage in trying to do a big service out there in the void." Many of those that maintained the *status quo* in their bailiwicks in 1932, 1933, and 1934, did so because they were able to serve effectively as insulators, and thereby cut off the currents of public opinion and discussion that were agitating the public mind in the outer world.

The Geography of "The Vote"

The party organization in Philadelphia is not equally strong in all sections of the city; its strength in any given neighborhood is likely to be determined (1) by the degree of want—which means poverty, ignorance, economic servitude of one sort or other—and (2) by the quality of leadership in the various sectors. In regard to the first of the two factors, one could go far, for example, in discovering in which areas the organization is particularly strong and in which ones it is moribund, by merely examining the several sections of the city from an airship. Houses surrounded by green lawns probably contain independent or semi-independent voters; the same is often true of houses in the most recently settled wards. Germantown in the Twenty-second Ward is old, but the houses stand alone and so do many of the voters in them. The Forty-second, Forty-ninth, Fiftieth, Thirty-eighth, and Thirty-fourth Wards are more recently developed and may be classed as semi-independent. All of the above wards, save the Thirty-eighth, which touches the Twenty-second and Forty-second Wards, are on the extreme edge of the city. They all contain the better residential districts, and only to a less extent districts and neighborhoods in which colored, foreign-born, and laboring people live. In the foreign-born and colored districts, on the other hand, the organization is almost certain to be strong and efficiently manned. For where there is a want (and there is certain to be one in the poorer districts), the party organization satisfies this want.

The human equation also enters in, of course; an indefatigable party worker produces results wherever he is, be it a silk-stocking district, silk and rayon, or only cotton. An economic interest, a tradition, a campaign appeal, or a compelling personality may also cause a division or a group of divisions to follow the organization ticket. Because of these less calculable factors, the bird's-eye view would not be 100 per cent accurate in locating all areas in which the party organization is strong; and yet it would be substantially correct.*

* The geography of the area and the relative wealth of its people are persuasive but not always the controlling factors in determining strongly organization-controlled divisions and wards. The strength of the organization is not confined to slum areas or divisions where the people are foreign born, colored, or living on a low economic plane (although it is most certain to be found in them). As I have said, the human factor must be considered here, just as it cannot be ignored in the sale of life insurance; an energetic and resourceful division leader may establish absolute control in a district that might normally tend toward independence. His problem is more difficult, but his results may be comparable to results obtained in some of the most effectively manned divisions of the first twenty wards. Sammy Dunbar's division is a case in point. Mr. Dunbar is chief clerk of the Mercantile Appraiser's office, and former chairman of the Forty-sixth Ward committee. He was formerly secretary to Penrose and later one of Grundy's key men in Philadelphia. In June, 1933, he was Vare's choice for the City Committee. In recent intra-party fights he carried his division for his faction each time and for his party even in 1932 and 1933. His division borders on Cobbs Creek Park at the very western end of the Forty-sixth Ward, and his people are substantially well off. The number of Sammy Dunbars in

Generally speaking, the strongly controlled wards are the first twenty; this is true of many cities besides Philadelphia. These are always the oldest wards. Here the most cultured people once lived, but now they have gone to outlying wards or the suburbs; in their places business and other commercial enterprises are flourishing, and on the fringe of this business zone one finds apartments and rooming houses, "the band-box area," and vice. In this old section one also finds an undue proportion of the foreign born, colored, and wage-earners. The objective facts indicate that this is the core of the party organization's strength. If a few of the other wards are nearly as completely under organization control as these first twenty it is the result of either one or both of two factors: (1) the personality and work of some great leader like Blakely McCaughn, Dave Hart, Billy Campbell, Johnny Dugan, Sheriff Weglein, John McKinley, or Clarence Crossan; or (2) the sentiment and associations of the people of the newer wards. For example, what was once the First Ward in Philadelphia has been divided into the Twenty-sixth, Thirty-sixth, Thirty-ninth, and Forty-eighth Wards. The organization is strong in all of these newer wards save the Twenty-sixth, and more recently the Forty-eighth. In these cases the weakness is temporary and is the result of ineffective leadership at the top. But it is the first wards that are usually the banner areas in city organization. For example, in the acid test of November, 1933,

---

Philadelphia is limited and they usually fail in the 1933's, but wherever one is found he is likely to be the controlling factor in his area in all but the elections in which the electorate is highly aroused.

58

when the Philadelphia organization suffered the most crushing defeat that it has experienced during the adult life of the oldest stalwart, it was victorious in the Thirty-ninth Ward and all the first twenty save the Fifteenth, Eighteenth, and Nineteenth. Moreover, the vote was close in the Eighteenth Ward, and also in the Twenty-seventh, Thirtieth, and Forty-seventh. The organization lost the Twenty-ninth Ward by fewer than fifty votes and the Twenty-fourth by less than a hundred. (The Twenty-fourth, Twenty-seventh, and Twenty-ninth results are due to effective organization leadership. The Thirtieth contains nearly three times as many colored as white people; it was lost to the organization through internal dissension. There are 4,716 native-born whites, 4,351 colored people, and 906 foreign-born whites in the Forty-seventh Ward.) Moreover, the strength of the organization is not confined to any particular wards—there are division strongholds in both the semi-organization wards and independent wards in varied sections of the city that the organization carried even in 1933.

When voters quit the first twenty wards they often leave a homogeneous neighborhood for one marked with heterogeneity. Close ties are broken; the majority of citizens moving to the freer air of West Philadelphia or Germantown will be affected by the voting habits of the electorate in their new environment. Some of them will discover that their ballots belong exclusively to themselves. The organization will be forced to work more strenuously to keep the voter *regular* after he has migrated. And in many cases the organization will fail

59

in this attempt. Its power is therefore being permanently weakened by the decreasing size of its feudal kingdom.

The extent of this population drift from the older wards may be seen by examining the following table; the statistics are taken from the official census returns for the years indicated.

Census	Population of first 20 wards	Population of the whole city	Per cent
1900	490,869	1,293,697	37.9
1910	497,300	1,549,008	32.1
1920	447,270	1,823,779	24.5
1930	364,214	1,950,961	18.6

In regard to the second factor influencing the strength of the organization, in no political area, no matter how small, does the division leader stand alone. Whether or not this ward organization is strong or weak may depend a good deal on the character of its general leadership rather than on its component parts, *i.e.*, the individual ward committeemen. If the ward leader is a man of discernment and truth and has a desire to strengthen his organization, he is almost certain to succeed in building up a fine spirit of loyalty among his men—true morale—and a group normally invincible in peace or war. The percentage of strong producers on his committee will be high; these individuals have every incentive to do their best. They know that good work will be recognized. Such conditions obtain in the

Twenty-fourth Ward; it is an excellent example of what one man, Blakely McCaughn, did during the period of his leadership to make a weak, unstable ward solidly "organization." A near-by ward with many of the same nationality and religious groups and economic and cultural classes, one that could well be as easily controlled for the organization as the Twenty-fourth, is uncertain in primaries and elections. This is due chiefly to the character of its leadership. The leader is not a man of his word, his promises are easily given and broken; he is so definitely a man of sporting proclivities that his attention wavers from politics. His appointments are so frequently given for personal rather than political reasons that many men leave this ward committee and go where their services will not be forgotten. Because morale is lacking in this organization, less than 40 per cent of the committeemen are strong producers—that is, are capable of carrying their divisions in any fight. The average committeemen may say, "Why should I work and serve the people? I get no credit—the leader appoints a relative or friend to the City Hall jobs." The ambitious committeeman here can attempt to align himself with some force outside his ward, or he can move away to the ward of a great leader, or he can just drift along. The statement that everyone in politics is influenced by everyone else in politics is particularly true of the division leader—ward leader relation.

If one asks the opinion of an old-time politician on the number of "real" committeemen there are in the 1,283 divisions, he is likely to say, "Study the primary returns; wherever a man controls his division time after time, he is real. The loafers can't last. If a man consecutively wins in his division, he is a producer. Votes don't just happen; they are given in return for service. You can pick out the effective committeemen by the vote they get." Then he will probably add that the highest percentage of real committeemen is in the South Philadelphia wards—Vare's original stronghold—or in the first twenty wards. But there is no ward in which there are not some strong committeemen; it is simply that the percentage is very much smaller in the semi-independent wards of west and northwest Philadelphia, and higher in the downtown wards.

As to the knowledge that a voter has of his ward committeeman, that varies in direct ratio to the strength of the party organization in a vicinity. If one asks a voter in the first five wards to name his committeeman, he might be told in the First Ward Peter Romagano, in the Second Frank Willard, in the Third Mike Foglietta, in the Fourth Nathan Ciplet, and in the Fifth Louie Silverstein; whereas if one makes a similar inquiry in one of the four or more semi-independent wards, he is likely to be told that the voter doesn't know—"I only see him at election time." Or conversely, one might meet a committeeman from one of the organization wards, in City Hall, and ask him when he has last served a voter in his division. He will usually give some such answer as "This morning," or "I am going to see Magistrate X or Judge Y or the probation officer or the mercantile appraiser now, about a matter for one of my people." An itemized statement of a real committeeman's services may require thirty minutes or an hour to relate, as I shall show in my individual sketches at the end of this section. But a committeeman from a semi-independent ward will answer this question by saying, "Last week," or "Last month," or "Two months ago," or "Never." He may not mean anything in the daily lives of the people in his division. He probably does not know them, and they do not know him. When these people are confronted with some difficulty they consult a lawyer or appeal directly to a public-relief committee, or, if they once lived in an organization ward, they are likely to call on their old committeeman for aid and comfort. Some of these "expatriates" from organization wards quite enjoy the free air of West Philadelphia, but others are at first surprised and then a bit resentful that no committeeman calls on them in their new home.

It is a nice question, whether the division leaders are inactive in many divisions in semi-independent wards because the people there tend toward independence—*i.e.*, can largely satisfy their own wants—or whether the people in these areas vote according to their own free will because the committeeman neglects to serve them. Both factors enter into the answer, but the former contains the clue to the explanation. Not everyone is capable of intellectual independence; this mental state is necessarily posited upon a degree of culture or intelligent interest in the common good, and a measure of economic independence. If these are lacking, the probability is that the individual will be apt to sacrifice his vote in order to satisfy a material want. If a man has no intellectual power of his own, he naturally takes the nearest leader—he has no desire for expressing a choice

63

involving factors he cannot see. It is also true that faithful service is bound to be recognized at election time, regardless of the neighborhood, but that the people living in the better residential districts have fewer wants; the committeeman has correspondingly fewer people to serve and fewer votes that he can call his own. A smile and ingratiating ways will go far even here, but of course they are not the stuff of which votes of the vintage of 1933 and 1934 are fashioned.

Conclusions

My description of ward committeemen is based primarily on the approximately four hundred "real" division leaders in the organization—the most active and resourceful of the 2,566 men elected to the party committee. These professional politicians are doing work that the official government, the city, the state, and the nation are not doing under our present social system. (This statement is more descriptive of the political arrangements existing before the great depression than of the present relation of citizen, politician, and official government.) And in the human way in which these little fellows in politics do their job, they are the world's greatest psychologists; they help in distress without taking on any airs of superiority or condescension. They are the kind friend for the moment rather than the wise one for the future. They are the missionairies who do not, even as an afterthought, ask the voter to reform.

It goes without saying that the social work done by the division leader is unscientific. His outdoor relief

64

might well keep a man dependent all his life, and make it very difficult for him ever to become properly adjusted socially. And he keeps people out of jail that probably should be in jail, when an enlightened social policy requires that society be considered as well as the plea of the individual who has been trapped. But the rights of society as a whole are of little or no concern to the average division leader. Only an individual can cry out in pain, and only an individual can vote. Probably the most serious criticism that can be brought against the politicians is that they believe that the government, like the vote, is theirs. They have given their life energy, their cash, their time to their little corner of the political world, and they have never been trained to look beyond that particular portion of it that is their own.

Furthermore if these "political philanthropists" were intelligently and sincerely interested in helping their people they would exert every effort toward establishing and maintaining both efficient and honest government in their city, for, as R. Fulton Cutting once remarked, good government is the greatest and best of all philanthropies because it touches 100 per cent of the population of the community. However, this is as foreign to the thinking of the professional politicians as would be the idea to the citizens that the members of a party committee should be paid a salary solely because they are doing social service work in their political bailiwicks. And yet if the division leader is a democratic Jack-of-all-trades doing a variety of services that people urgently want done, it might be wise public policy, in so far as his work is lawful in nature, to put him on the public pay roll. The best of the party workers and leaders are there now through a legal fiction. England has officially recognized the public value of an opposite political party, by putting its leader on the public pay roll, as the guiding force of His Majesty's opposition. This illustration bears on the present discussion only to the extent that it is an example of a party leader's receiving a public salary exclusively because of the value of his work as party leader. Our party leaders usually receive salaries, too, but only when they hold some make-believe positions in the official government. It would make for sanity in public life if positions were awarded on the basis of merit, and if the official government were either to do the social work that the most active division leaders do, or pay these "social workers" a living wage for doing it.

The element of barter is almost certain to come into our democratic scheme of things, for the United States government is "of the people"; and the generality of our people are barterers rather than idealists—they have a sense of commerce rather than a sense of state. And in the case of city politics, in its protoplasmic manifestations, the question might be asked, what real difference is there between a person who gives his vote for a two-dollar bill and one that trades it for a painfully needed basket of groceries or a discharge from a magistrate's court? And if either of these barters is a negation of the democratic spirit—and they both are—how can the wealthy manufacturer be described who gives not only his vote but also a $50,000 campaign contribution to the

66

political party that will enact a high tariff into law? As for the majority of division leaders, they think of themselves as the Robin Hoods of the city. Most of them are conscious of no wrongdoing. They blandly, and often arrogantly, assume that the votes and the magistrates belong to them. They are genial, friendly men even though they are probably insolent concerning their assumed prerogatives on election day. Service for votes is the cardinal tenet of their political philosophy.

The most common personality traits of these men are friendliness, energy, and resourcefulness. The born division leader also has enough imagination to be interested in his neighbor's problems. He likes people and he likes to serve them. He is happiest when he is in a group. He has no desire to be let alone. As for honesty, the division leaders are usually as honest as their respective constituencies. Those that remain on the party committee ten, twenty, thirty years, are representative of their people, and that is descriptive of American democracy. These men are the servants of the voters (and, in an important sense, their masters, too), but they are not the voters' preceptors in ethics.

The division leaders stand at the limit of the voters' attention—and it is true that the limit of the voters' attention is the limit of democracy. Many voters cannot see much beyond the division leader, and yet every time they vote they are called upon to express opinions and choices about the issues and men utterly beyond their leader in the outer world; issues and men beyond their own interests, and often beyond their comprehension. In following his ticket without question or discussion they substitute his views for their own. A substantial number of people are willing to do this for two reasons: first, because the leader is their friend, or one that can give or withhold favors; second, because in the majority of elections they have no strong reason for not voting his way. (For example, Al Smith was the first important candidate to get under the skins of the voters in South Philadelphia; however, by 1932 and 1933 the hardships of the great depression had caused the voter to view his franchise with more concern. Increasing numbers of citizens now want some "say" in marking their own ballot; many voters have come to believe that they can get more *service* by supporting the candidates of the party of the Democratic Roosevelt than they can get by continuing to follow the ticket of their Republican division leader. If this period of stress continues, and if the Senator from Louisiana does not stub his toe, some citizens will cast their ballot for Huey P. Long and his Share-the-Wealth Plan with the idea of exchanging a vote for $5,000.)

Whether or not the attitude of Philadelphia's two million inhabitants is permanently reoriented by the continuing impact of the great depression, party organization will remain as inevitable as the tides in the ocean. The size of this political community is too great to permit a collective opinion to be formed without the help of organization. The radio has again brought the actual state within the limits of the definition fixed by Aristotle, the father of political science; both Mussolini and Hitler have demonstrated its significance as an

68

agent of social control in lands where freedom of speech does not exist. Here freedom of speech does exist, but we are none the less beginning to see how effectively the radio can be used to arouse the citizens' interest in particular political leaders and programs. President Roosevelt, Senator Huey Long, or Father Coughlin plus a radio broadcast—in periods of stress—may be more potent, for a while, than an army of party workers. However, the basic task for either a national leader or the leader of a division or precinct is to contact the citizen in every community and to sell the party ticket to every potential voter. This suggests that in the long run the radio is a supplement to, rather than a substitute for, a hierarchy of party committees.

However, party organization is only an instrument, a means to an end, and an alert citizenry can force it to serve the common good just as an indifferent electorate may permit the organization to serve a private end. In a democracy there is no substitute for the right public attitude, and this in turn is directly related to the comparative prosperity of the people; to their social training and social vision; to the possession of common traditions, ideals, and language; to the length of their ballot and the reasonableness of the questions placed before the voter.

Lippmann once wrote, "You can beat Tammany Hall permanently in one way—by making the government of a city as human, as kindly, as jolly as Tammany Hall."

This statement is of great importance; in addition, the depression indicates that the government must be

69

useful (relieve economic distress) as well as jolly if it is to hold the favorable attention of the electorate. At the present time the Federal government as personified by Franklin Roosevelt is providing both the jobs and the smile. But the voter's memory is short, his eyesight is bad; all the facts indicate that he who holds public office for any length of time must establish face-to-face contact with the voter. In order to keep the government interested in the common good, public-spirited men and women will have to organize—even as the successful politicians organize—right down into the wards and precincts. And if the future brings higher standards of living, more leisure, more per capita goods, both necessities and luxuries, part of the voter's incentive to be interested in his government will be gone. This situation will increase the need for civic education, public discussion, and organization—organization in detail.

In the last analysis, the political party organization is a middleman. It achieves supremacy by granting small favors—economic, legal, and psychological—and it sells this political power to the controlling economic interests. As for the majority of individuals, it is impossible to have a political right without economic security. To them the vote is more a commodity than either a right or an obligation. The problem for the future is to help increasing numbers of citizens to identify their ballot with a sound program of social action on the part of the official government rather than as something to be neglected, to be cast according to some whim, or to be given to a friend.

70

And in conclusion, one may observe that politics is, as the French say, *une tranche de la vie*—a slice of life. One's attitude toward it is inextricably connected with his basic attitude toward the larger questions of the development of his own personality, his religion, and his life.

II
SKETCHES

●

TONY NICOLLO

HARRY ROTHSCHILD

TOM COLE

TIMOTHY FLANAHAN

SAM TERNBERG

GEORGE KENDALL

NICHOLAS FISHBOURNE

DAVID NELSON

ROSIE POPOVITS

TONY NICOLLO

The People's Friend

TONY NICOLLO's division has one vacant lot, five hundred
and twenty-two souls, and three hundred and four votes.
Three hundred and two of these votes he counts as his
own, and the other two he concedes to the opposition.
He is a short, stockily built Italian-American in his
early thirties, with small hands and feet, and dark,
reddish hair, thinning to baldness on the crown; he is
an ex-prize fighter, featherweight. He has had no
education beyond that which he got in the elementary
schools, but his father says that as a boy he was more
given to staying at home and listening to political
discussions than to running around with the other boys.
His face is expressive and genial, and his eyes are respon-
sive and alert. He is singularly literate for one of his
training and background, and when he talks he shows
no trace of his Italian parentage. His father was for
twenty years a division leader before him, and Tony
himself is one of the shrewdest of the many that I know.

He lives in a river ward where the organization is very
strong. When he moved into this ward at the time of his
marriage in 1924, he proceeded to vote, but found that a
lot of his relatives were not voting. He asked them why,
and they answered that the ballot did not mean anything

to them—besides, no one ever came to ask them to go to the polling place. He also noticed that the leadership in this division was so ineffective that nearly half the voters were Democrats. He thought that was strange. Added to this was the further fact that no one came to him when he voted.

At this time he was a piano salesman; the radio business was increasing, and he began wondering how long the piano business was going to hold out. He then got the idea of becoming a politician. He got a friend to take him to Jimmie, the ward leader. Jimmie asked what he wanted, and he said that he wanted to become a division leader in his division. Jimmie said, "Oh, no, the leaders are made by the people." Tony answered that he wanted to be the organization division leader and that he wanted to be recognized by the powers in the Republican party. The ward leader replied, "I don't care what happens in that division. It is often against me. I was thinking of moving a strong division leader down there." The young Italian said, "You won't need to. We [Italians] are able to take care of ourselves down there." The ward leader then said, "Well, you show me what you can do."

Two years later there was a factional fight. Tony was asked to go along with the group opposing Vare, the Boss. He refused, and said that he was standing by Vare. His conversation on the subject was repeated to his leader, Jimmie. Jimmie later asked him where he stood in the matter of the fight. (This was the factional fight in the Republican party between Senator Pepper and Congressman Vare for the United States Senate. Jimmie

76

was Vare's ward leader for his particular ward.) The Italian's partner had said that Vare had no chance for winning in their division. Jimmie looked at the Italian and expressed his great confidence in him by saying, "You go down there and run that division. Take care of everything." And the leader's choice was ratified at the next election; Tony was made a bona fide division leader.

Since that time Tony has been the dominant leader in this constituency. Some of his experiences as leader I will relate in his own words.

"I picked out the election officials for this campaign. They were men that were loyal to me—that is, they would do what I told them on election day. Two of the four election officials that I picked were Jewish, in spite of the fact that there were only ten Jews in the division. I picked them because of their ability. I then got a watcher's certificate. [This certificate enables the person holding it to be present at the polling place at the time of election.] I saw to it that all of my family voted, and all my relatives. This counted for fifteen votes. I persuaded some women who had never before voted to vote at this election. As a result of my special work I got two hundred and ninety-seven people registered. That was more than a hundred more than usually registered before my time. Jimmie was so well pleased with my registration work that he put my name on the public pay roll. I was a typist in the Recorder of Deeds office, although I could hardly type. Six months later I was appointed assistant chief lien clerk. Then a few months later Jimmie asked me if I wanted to be inspector in the

Bureau of Weights and Measures. Everybody wants a
job in this department, because it gives you more time
to serve your people. [In certain positions a few hours a
day or week are all that one must give to his official
duties at City Hall, and the rest of the time he is free
for serving the people in his division, and doing all the
other things that a young politician might want to do.]
A few months ago I was transferred to the district
attorney's office. My work here is more difficult and
requires much time, but I accepted this place because
I want to know the right people. I am thinking of the
future. [The salary for each of these places is $1,800 a
year.]

"Many of my voters come to my home to ask favors.
You ought to come around some night. My father can
tell you. Sometimes they sit there and I sit in the next
room at my desk and take them one by one just like a
doctor. My wife is not so much interested in all the
people as I am, and I tell her that she must always smile
at everyone. I must never look cross either. And I must
be careful that my children avoid friction by not hitting
other children. I must not let my children think that
they are superior to any children in the neighborhood or
the division. I must also watch out for arguments between neighbors. I never intercede in trouble of this sort.
In handling a division you must read people's minds.
Some you must bully; some you are nice to; some you
must buy; some you coax; some you threaten; and others
you can make happy by taking them for a ride in your
automobile."

78

I had a list of the names and addresses of the 367 assessed voters in this division, and I called the names of seven people listed here in order to find out if the division leader could tell me exactly where they lived. He gave the correct address for six, and one he missed by a single door.

This division leader and other successful party workers substantiate Ratzenhofer's statement that a political party meets an incarnate want. Tony meets an incarnate want by serving the people in such a way that they are willing to vote as the party dictates on election day During one conversation with Tony I asked him to enumerate the concrete favors he had done for his constituents within the last twenty-four hours. Here are some of them:

"John R. needed a job. He wanted a letter of reference to the Sage Brush Oil Co. I wrote a letter on the stationery of the Philadelphia City Council and got Jimmie to sign it.

"Candloror G. in bad shape and wanted help from the Dodge committee. [This committee is a charitable organization for those Philadelphians who are utterly destitute—that is, living on the disaster level.] I sent a letter to the Dodge committee, urging them to provide food stuffs for this person.

"Pietro K. came to me in order to get some money for food. I sent a letter to the Dodge committee for help.

"I sent for the automobile license for two people.

"I have a dozen other examples here of recent services. Here are some of them.

"A few nights ago one of my people sent for me. I immediately went to the house from which the call came. A little girl let me in. She said, 'My mother wants you. She is upstairs in bed.' I hesitated and then I went up. There the mother was with a new baby. She told me that she had nothing and that the baby was dying of want. She wanted to know if I would bury the baby if it died. I told her that I thought the city would. I went to see Jimmie at once. We sent a stiff letter to the Dodge committee. This committee replied that these people had been getting six dollars a week since December, and had received medical attention. They did not know about the baby, however. I mention this case particularly because people sometimes try to take advantage of the division leader, and get everything they can for nothing.

"Sunday I received no requests for food or things of that sort, but I was at the station house three times. [When a constituent of an organization ward, in particular, gets arrested for some minor crime or misdemeanor, his first thought is likely to be to get in touch with his division leader, who will go to the station house, obtain a technical copy of the charge, take this to a friendly magistrate who will sign it for the leader, provided the charge is not murder or some crime of equal seriousness, and the leader will take the "copy" back to the station house where the man is in custody, and secure his release. He will be told when to appear for a hearing before the magistrate, and then again, at the hearing, the committeeman will intercede for him, and will probably secure his discharge, or, if there is some

80

obstacle to prevent that, he will soften the blow of the law that would otherwise fall directly upon his constituent. One need not spend a lifetime in any of the great American cities to understand why the majority of individuals saved from a night in a cell or from a prison sentence would have a genial feeling toward the person who had effected the release!] People go out in the edge of the city where there are open spaces. They think they are out in the country. One of my men was shooting birds on Forest Avenue! I had to get him out.

"I find that politicians are very jealous. We are apt to wish that those holding superior positions were dead, and also to very quickly resent any advantage that is given to our fellow-workers and not to us."

Shortly after Tony started in politics he made an agreement with two leaders in adjacent divisions. One was a resourceful Jewish lawyer and the other was a genial, old-time politician in the sheriff's office. These men help each other; if one cannot appear at a magistrate's hearing or does not know the right person in one of the courts or city departments, the other speaks for him.

"In summer I get a permit card every year to open a fire plug. Fifty or sixty children come under it. There are few baths in my division. The permit is from Chief Jones of the Bureau of Water. It authorizes me to open the fire hydrants and equip them with sprinklers.

"Here is a family of three Italians who never voted. The boy is a garage mechanic. One night he started to fix a car at the owner's house, and had to take it to his garage. He was arrested on his way back. Police asked to see his license. He had none. His mother came to me. I said, 'Why should I help you? You never vote. No. I won't help you.' Then the father came, and he gave me a hard luck story. I told him that I would not run around town to help him—he never did anything for me. Finally they both came. Then I told them that I would help. I got the boy out on a copy of the charge. The family said that they would always vote. They registered and then came to me after registration. They looked as if they were in trouble. The man said, 'My God, Tony, I don't know what to do!' 'What's the matter?' I said. 'We want to go to the country, and won't be able to vote!' he said. 'Here now,' I said, 'That's different. If you are going away, or if you are sick, that's different. The only thing I don't like is to have you here and not vote. But if you must go away, that's all right. I'll be for you just the same!'—and they went away feeling relieved.

"Beno Cellani pays a $3.50 support order for a child that he thinks he's not the father of. He wanted to fight the order. I took him to Martin's office for free legal advice. Martin advised him to go on since he had pleaded guilty. He pays now and feels all right about it.

"My people that own homes must pay taxes, of course. I tell them when the taxes are due, and in many cases I deliver the tax bills and try to get the people to pay in advance and save the three per cent the city gives those that pay their taxes before a certain date.

"Some of my people are funny. I have done five or six favors for some of them, and then they will say, 'What did you ever do for us?' Even that saloon keeper

82

that I saved from going to jail or paying a fine, said, 'What did you ever do for me?' You could do a hundred favors for a person and fail on the last one, and lose his support at election. [Tony is cynical concerning gratitude in the human heart.] 'Don Ward used to give each one of his party committeemen $20 at Christmas time. Now that he has fallen, his friends have all run away from him. Gratitude!!' But the majority of people are not like that. The Italian people are most grateful of all. Sometimes they tip their hats to me as I pass them on the street—the old men and all. They think I am someone big. They like to talk to me and to be seen in my company."

Although one of Tony's chief duties is to keep people out of jail, occasionally he helps to put one in. Not long ago an American family of three women moved into his neighborhood. "Soon after they came," said Tony, "I was told that there were a lot of goings on between the colored men and these white women. My people thought it wasn't a nice thing on a small street like this where children were growing up. I didn't pay much attention at first. Later, however, one night I sent for this white woman and she came in to see me and sat right there where the wife is, and I told her just what I had heard. I told her that this neighborhood wouldn't stand for it. This woman was about twenty-five I judge, and rather nice-looking. I told her that if she didn't watch herself her house would be raided. I thought it only fair to warn her. She finally said, 'Well, I'm glad you are telling me. I'll see what I can do.' Last Monday night a man came around and began to complain that

83

we had to do something. 'All right,' I said, 'You tell me when they are there.' About eleven o'clock he came back and said, 'You can get them now.' I called the police captain—of course he knows me—they came in a little red wagon with six or seven officers. Some went to the front, some went around to the back, and one raps on the door. Sure enough, a woman pops her head out the window and says, 'What do you want?' 'We want to search the house,' he said. 'All right, we'll be down in a minute.' Then they heard a lot of running down stairs, for being a small house like this, for instance, you can hear everything. And sure enough the white woman came out the front to see what they wanted and at the same time the colored men were going out the back with their pants and shoes in their hands. They were all arrested and taken to the police station. There were four colored men and four white women, all put in the same patrol wagon and taken to 17th and X street. The extra woman was an Italian and married. She began to cry, 'My husband will kill me!' and all that. This woman was about thirty—a sort of stout, chunky woman. About eleven-thirty I gets the first call from this fellow in the station house. I had always taken care of him before. He was always a nice fellow until these white women moved in. I always tried to get him work and little odd jobs—things like that. The phone rang and he said, 'Is Mr. Tony there?' I said, 'What do you want?' 'Tell him Tom W. wants him.' 'Well, Tony is not at home, and you won't get him till morning.' 'Well, you see if you can get in touch with him and let him know about me.' I said, 'All right.' The next

84

morning about seven, the phone rang. I had her [his wife] answer it. She said, 'He will be at the magistrate's hearing.' He said, 'Are your sure?'. . . . So I goes down to the station house and this colored fellow expected me to intercede for him, but instead I got ahold of the magistrate and told him I wanted those people to get the limit. The judge gave them three months each in the house of correction. And now I just got this letter from this colored fellow to try to help him.

Tony Nicollo
————STREET, PHILADELPHIA

Tony, I am in the house of correction. I got three months. I was caught in a raid and please try to get me a special discharge as soon as possible as I am expecting my wife to come out of the hospital in about a week or so and I won't be home to take care of her and let me know at once what you can do for me, Tony. Will you tell Mary Smith to take care of my house and take the dog out of the cellar and tell Mary to go to 845 S. Street and get the door key for the house and tell Mary to look in my coat pocket and get the hospital visiting card and go to the hospital to see Sue on visiting day for me and write me and let me know how she is getting along at once. Tony, do what you can for me at once, please. Yours,

Tom Washington, #55

Tony's people appreciate him so much that they like to stay near him. "What are the boundaries of your division, Tony?" asked one voter. "I want to move, but I want to stay in your division." One woman told him that her husband would not get out of Tony's division even though she had wanted to move for two years to a better house.

Theoretically division leaders receive no pay, but they have a job at City Hall, the duties of which are not too exacting, or they have some business or other connection that is helped by their activity in party politics. However, it is beyond the powers of human nature to submerge oneself always in the service of the party. Some committeemen accept silver and gold for the more valuable of their services, but not Tony. To him all service is done for the vote, yet some of his grateful constituents will not be content with giving just the vote. Every now and then he receives a chicken from some person whom he has befriended, or a clock, or a finely tailored suit, or some other gifts of the kind. And each year he is given, all told, more than a barrel of wine. The wine of life to Tony, however (he does not drink), is to walk down the mean, narrow street on which he lives and speak to the people sitting on the steps. No king ever surveyed his realm with greater satisfaction.

86

HARRY ROTHSCHILD

A University Man in Politics

❮❮❮-❮❮❮

"I WILL not be able to deliver a banner division in the Nth Ward in 1934 without taking care of these eight mercantile taxes now. I must help this person that was arrested for a traffic violation, too. If you want a complete record of what I spend on election day, both in time and money and energy, you must add this and other things in. I work every day in the week for my people, and I never refuse to see a caller or answer my telephone, regardless of the hour. In fact, a call after official office hours is usually more urgent than one between nine and five." So spoke Harry Rothschild, an energetic and promising young ward committeeman, a university graduate, still in his twenties. He is also a successful attorney with an income of more than $5,000. Seven years ago he studied political parties at the University of Pennsylvania, but he had thought of politics long before he met his university professors. He was intelligent, industrious, and well prepared in the classroom; of the seventy-odd students, he and two others led all the rest in their grasp of the subject matter, and their ability to ask important questions. His senior research was a first-hand interview with each of the forty-eight ward leaders. He managed to see thirty-six of them himself;

from the director of the City Committee he obtained data concerning the others. Today he knows them all, and there are few young university men of whom this can be said. Then as now he was handsome—an athletic type, blond, with good color, perfect teeth, distinguished features, and a gracious, winsome smile. Most interesting of all, he has "the common touch." One senses it in talking to him and in watching him talk to others. Whether he is talking to a sedate gentleman in the Manufacturer's Club, or an old-time politician in City Hall that never quite made the grade, he is friendly, natural, and courteous. I never fully realized how universal his appeal was until I talked to Joe Cobb in City Hall. (He is the office boy for three important politicians, the county commissioners. He sits on a chair behind a small desk that is just within the door of the anteroom. Any ordinary person that wants to see Jimmie Clark, John O'Donnell, or Johnny Dugan, must see Joe first. He weighs 305 pounds and he is not tall. He is built like the diamond on the ace of diamonds—his paunch is big, his head, feet, and hands are small. He has lived in two places within a stone's throw of each other for forty years. I asked if he were not tired of living in one neighborhood so long. He replied that once he had told his father that they were going to move away from the Tenth, and his father had said, " 'The only way that I will go away from here is in a pine box.' My mother said the same. Now I'll never leave it either." Mr. Cobb is a ward committeeman and entered politics through the police force. "I got active in politics as soon as I went on the police force. I went around the polling

88

place on election day and I learnt a plenty. You learnt quick and you learnt plenty. When a man appoints you to the police force, you are for him." He repeated the committeeman's catechism with a variation: "Know your people, get acquainted, be ready to get up at three or four o'clock in the morning to sign a copy of the charge. You ask what the copy is for. You are told drunkenness. You get to the station house and find that it ain't that at all. It's drunkenness while driving a car, driving without a license, and larceny of an automobile. Then I know that I might as well go back home. No magistrate will let a man out on those charges without bail." He breathed a sigh, relief or regret—I do not know which—and remarked that he just couldn't tell me "about the early days in politics, when the police took a hand—it wouldn't look right in a book!") One day he did say, "Harry is a fine boy—he is doing well in politics. He makes his mark."

Not long ago an important state official gave Harry a coveted appointment. One politician that might have received it, but did not, expressed the viewpoint of many when he said, "Well, if I can't have the appointment, I would rather see Harry get it than anyone I know." Harry's work in this connection is with certain banks that have been closed by the state. His appointment was no sooner made than he enrolled in an evening class at the Wharton School of the University in order to study banking and consult with the faculty. (Adding this technical course to a busy life nicely reveals the quality of this politician. The majority of individuals might have thought their training adequate since the appointment had already been made—but not Harry. His idea is to do the job in hand as well as it can be done.)

"A lawyer wanted a hearing postponed, I knew the magistrate and easily arranged it. Now I can count on him." So spoke Harry on one occasion, and went on to make a more general statement about the work that he does for his constituents. "I always do more than ten favors a week for my people, and sometimes the number is greater than twenty. I have about three station-house cases a week; 90 per cent of them are traffic matters. I have never charged anyone in my division a cent for legal services. I am willing to go out of my way a darn sight more than the other lawyers in my ward. You can't be afraid of work and succeed in this game. If you stand on ceremony you can get no place—not in the sort of politics I am interested in. Several years ago I had first of all to decide whether I was going to stay in politics. I could already see that there might be things that a university man might not want to do. I decided that the type of people in my neighborhood would support a man that would honestly and efficiently serve them. Friendly and efficient service are the two big planks in my platform. The majority of my people are no more interested in having a bum for a committeeman than I am in being one. I think that they take pride in their representative on the ward committee. That is one way of interpreting our never-failing vote.

"I am interested only in ward politics at present because I feel that right now it is necessary for me to control at least one division so that I can have a definite standing in our party organization. It is merely an

90

interest and a means to an end and not one that I entirely enjoy. However, I don't want you to feel that I consider myself too good for a job as ward committeeman. I do not forget that George Welsh was a member of the Ward Committee of the Twenty-fourth Ward during his entire career as a Congressman and up until the date of his election to the Federal bench. As a matter of fact, his resignation from the Twenty-fourth Ward Committee was not accepted until a regular meeting of the Twenty-fourth Ward Committee, more than a month after he had been serving on the bench.

"I first got interested in politics during my second year in high school. I got into the debates concerning party candidates, and I liked to talk politics. In my junior and senior years I branched out in class politics and got elected to committees, and I helped elect my friends to them. When I reached the University I was a full-fledged politician." At the end of his first year in the University he had formed an alliance with three other men which lasted throughout the rest of his college career. One of them represented a certain fraternity group, another a dormitory group, the other a different fraternity group, while Harry represented the Philadelphians. Together they managed to manipulate the political affairs of their class. As Harry says, if he gets as close to running Philadelphia as he got to running his class at Penn, he will become President of City Council!

To go on with his experiences as a boy in connection with Philadelphia politics: "I was still in high school when I stuck Congressman X's posters up on telephone poles. At that time [1919], we lived in the Thirty-second

Ward. The Jewish people were just moving into that section. There were two Jews running for the ward committee. I was fifteen, and I got interested in their campaign. I talked to eight or ten friends about them. The one that I was most interested in lost, but he was elected two years later. However, I had a scrap with him over a fellowship that I wanted and didn't get. I was not active in his successful contest. I got a job on a neighborhood newspaper when I was finishing high school and after. This gave me more influence, for I wrote articles or news items about our section of the city. About this time I used to go around to the William K. Evans Republican Club [the local club named after a councilman that later became a judge]. There I met the politicians—some big ones like Councilman W and Al Lichenstein, now leader of the ward.

"In 1922 I helped the committeemen in my division get votes for Beidleman [candidate for the gubernatorial nomination]. About this time I became city editor on our neighborhood paper. It had five thousand circulation. In 1925 my family moved to my present ward. I got immediately into division politics although I was not old enough to vote until 1926. I worked for Judge Glass in 1925, and Vare in 1926. I canvassed my division. This was when I began making speeches, in the spring of 1926. I spoke before women's clubs and other organizations in behalf of the Vare candidacy. Pepper men won for the ward committee, but Vare carried the ward. One of these committeemen went to California in 1926. I was appointed to the vacancy caused in the party committee. I knew the people. Pat McGrath, vice-chairman of the

92

committee, a tipstaff, and an old veteran who had taken
an interest in me, nominated me at a meeting of my
ward executive committee, and Judge Black, the ward
leader, sanctioned my appointment. At the next election
in 1928 I was elected to the ward committee, and I was
again elected in 1930."

Harry was reelected in 1932, and at that time his
division, which is one of the wettest in Philadelphia,
had the banner vote in all the city for General Butler,
the governor's dry candidate. Senator Davis beat the
General in the city by several hundred thousand votes.
The General's victory in this one division is a tribute to
his young and popular lieutenant. Harry's people were
no more interested in Pinchot's candidate and the dry
issue than are the majority of Philadelphians in the
city at large. But he worked for Butler throughout the
entire eight divisions of his district. In addition, because
of his personal friendship for Judge Stadtfeld, candidate
for the superior court, he organized several groups for
him and had representatives in many of the divisions in
Philadelphia, especially where there was any considerable Jewish vote to work for him. Harry supported
Butler like a good soldier—he has a job under the
governor, and he has no intention of resigning at this
time. Although he obtained his position in part because
of his character and training, it requires more than that
to keep it when the governor or his friends campaign for
public office.

One of the most important things in Harry's political
career to date has been his connection with the party
organization's newspaper. One can easily understand

93

the desire of many of the politicians, whether high or low, to have their names in print. It is by write-ups of this sort that he is able to get a great many of his favors done. For instance, Magistrate X is the ———— court judge. There are a dozen and one things that he is interested in having other people know he is doing; in other words, he is not at all disinclined to having his many varied activities "played up." He will call Harry from time to time on some of these particular matters and Harry sees that they get into print. As a result when a friend of Harry's goes into court all he has to do is to tell the judge that he is a friend of Harry's and the effect is magical (though the reasons for this effect are usually unknown to the constituent).

As a matter of fact, if Harry were to weigh the advantages he gets out of being ward committeeman (especially in the Nth Ward with the type of ward leader he has there), as against the contacts and things that he can get done as a result of his connection with the political journal, he would find that probably 80 per cent of his favors are accomplished by reason of the paper and 20 per cent by reason of his membership on the ward committee. This is really the most essential part of his political life at present. In addition he makes numerous contacts through organizations to which he belongs; these stand him in good stead when he has to ask favors for his constituents. He does not join the organizations merely for political reasons, for he really enjoys work in these groups, but he does not hesitate to take advantage of the connections thus established if they will benefit his people. After all, they are interested in results and they

94

do not care whether he gets them because of his membership in the ward committee or in some other organization; or because he does a little writing now and then for the political journal; or because he is well acquainted with the lieutenant governor through a personal friend of his; or because by reason of his legal training he is able to advise them on a business matter which is troubling them. What they do know and care about is that he does get results.

One day's casual list of services that Harry cited for me once was as follows: "I took care of one traffic notice before Magistrate X. I arranged through my friend [a business man with political influence] for another one of my constituents to be discharged for a violation of a traffic ordinance in Fairmount Park. I wrote a letter for one of my constituents who is about to be sued by a former workman for wages, explaining to this workman's lawyer why no wages were due. I saw the son of Magistrate Z about a hearing which is to come up before his father tomorrow morning. It appears that one of my constituents is a contractor and he employed a plumber who was not registered, thus violating either knowingly or unknowingly the sanitation code. Tomorrow he must appear to answer and ostensibly to pay a fine. Jimmie will use his good offices with his father tonight, and I have given this fellow a card to hand to the judge at the hearing tomorrow reminding him that this was the case his son talked to him about. I interviewed one of the real-estate assessors with reference to the reduction of an assessment. He turned me down cold and I will therefore probably have to file an appeal.

"I interviewed this afternoon a number of political factors including your friend a magistrate's clerk with reference to taking care of a traffic violation in Rockledge, which is a little borough in Montgomery County about ten miles out of Philadelphia. Nobody seems to know that particular Justice of the Peace and they were therefore unable to help me, and this goes for your friend the clerk. I therefore communicated with one of my school friends, now one of the assistant district attorneys in Montgomery County, in this matter, and I think he will be able to straighten it out for me.

"You may remember that this Christmas at the request of Father X, who is the priest of the parish that includes my district, I supplied him with about fifteen special baskets for some of his needy constituents. This of course goes quite a way toward gathering the Catholic vote."

Harry Rothschild is too well-balanced a person to be described by any one personality trait. However, like a good many of the politicians, his one most striking quality is his energy. He is always on the go; he craves action, purposeful action, rather than even a degree of quiet. His official duties, his legal work, his political services require more than the sum total of the average person's time and industry. Yet for Harry these interests are but the core of his life. In addition he plays nine holes of golf twice each week when the weather is favorable. In the winter he devotes a similar amount of time to handball or swimming. He confines his smoking almost entirely to banquets, dinners, and luncheons that he attends—but there are many of these festive occasions. He does not drink.

96

He is too restless and ambitious to sit around City Hall and talk for long stretches of time. Other men do just that; they go there because they like to loaf around in that atmosphere. But usually one can enumerate exactly the reasons that take Harry to this Mecca. All his trips to City Hall, except when they are made entirely because of legal matters he is handling, are for political purposes of an explicit sort. Let me list some concrete instances that are typical of the things he has to do there.

On one occasion he had to give a good deal of his time to a case in which one of his constituents, a shoemaker, was involved. The shoemaker had tried to make a little money on the side by running a still in his second-story apartment. Unfortunately for him, the odors, even though pleasant, of a fifty-gallon still in operation attracted the attention of some of the neighbors, who reported it to the police, and he was raided. Harry took care of him at the time he was arrested; he got him out on a copy of the charge, and had a low bail fixed for him. After Harry's plea to the court, the bootlegger was given a year's probation.

There was a tailor living near him who had a great deal of difficulty in passing his citizenship test, due to his unfamiliarity with the form of our government, etc. He was a very persevering individual, however, and until he had failed a good many times he was backward about calling attention to his failure or telling anyone about his efforts. Finally in despair, he came to see Harry. The gentleman in charge of immigration matters happened to be a friend of the Chief of the Income Tax Department, who, in turn, lived in Harry's division, and was a good friend of his. Between the two of them, they were successful in getting the tailor through the test so that he could become a full-fledged citizen. It is easy to guess how that man will vote when he has the opportunity to do so.

Another thing that Harry did as committeeman was to put through an ordinance whereby electric lights were put up at the end of driveways in his division so that people could more easily determine which were their own garages at night. He also met the wishes of a number of housewives in his division who wanted the streets and driveways sprinkled more frequently than the city was doing at this time. He went to the chief of the street-cleaning division for his part of the city and got the water wagon to run through his division one extra day a week, even though the wagon had to be brought quite a distance to do it.

A young doctor decided to locate in his division. Though the doctor knew a good many people in that section of the city, he was not quite sure of their addresses. He wanted to send announcements of the opening of his office throughout the whole district as well as to his friends. He came to Harry and asked him to get the assessor's list for him. Harry did this, though they were not easily obtained at that time. It was only because he had "the proper connections" in the County Commissioner's office that he was able to get the different lists.

One of his constituents was getting the "run-around" from one of the insurance carriers for her former employer. She had sustained an injury as a result of an

98

accident which occurred during her employment and the company refused to compensate her. Harry took it up with the Workmen's Compensation Referee in the District, who was a Pinchot appointee, and also with his secretary; these two were able to save about sixty days in the listing of the case. When the case was heard, Harry and his side were given all the "breaks," and the referee found for Harry's claimant. The insurance company did not feel it worth while to incur the enmity of the referee over this small matter of $90, but to the woman this was a lot of money, and the service of the committeeman was of great value to her.

Speaking of Harry's services to this young woman suggests another of his occasional services to his constituents. To quote him again, "I have had occasion to attend social affairs given in my community. I have made it my business at those affairs to single out some of the young ladies who might otherwise have been left warming their chairs, or standing with their backs to the ballroom walls, and give them an opportunity to loosen up those creaking joints. I didn't hesitate to apply these methods to some of the 'dowagers.' After all, if you can make votes with a dance, it is as good a method as taking care of traffic notices, etc. When they're in the box, one counts just as much as the other."

At certain times he is very much occupied with getting reductions in assessments for his constituents. The greatest part of this is on properties in his own division, but sometimes his people own property elsewhere, and he has to run around and see a number of assessors. If he cannot get a job done without an appeal, he

99

generally files an appeal which is heard before the Board of Revision; he must attend the hearing.

But even though these City Hall visits have so definite a purpose, that does not prevent Harry from blithely passing up and down the corridors or into offices, speaking and shaking hands with friends and acquaintances. He is something of an efficiency expert and politician combined, although primarily he is and thinks of himself as a lawyer.

Several times I have been with him at his home for dinner—a pleasant, comfortable house like the majority of the houses in his division. His excellent mother, a woman of the old school, prepared the dinners, and they were culinary achievements of the first order. These glimpses into his home life help me to understand why Harry is no ordinary politician or student, and also some of the reasons why he is still a single man.

While I was at his home I was always impressed again with the extraordinary busy-ness of his life. We always talked for an hour or so after dinner. This hour and the dinner hour were always broken into by telephone calls. At the end of the hour, he would usually explain that he had to see someone about some matter and he wondered if I would like to be first taken home in his car. One always feels the pressure of this work to be done when one is with him, and yet he never seems hurried or distracted or too busy to see people. And I know of no one who answers letters more painstakingly and with less regard to any possible gain thereby. In 1929 I sent him a question from Oklahoma, after having been away from Philadelphia for three years. He immediately replied in a closely written communication of more than nine hundred pertinent words. Since then I have received more than twenty informing and delightful letters in response to questions asked, and the majority of these documents are of four hundred words or more in length. I commented on this one time, and he replied that he tried to answer his correspondence immediately and that he noticed that the best politicians did likewise; he cited Congressman Welsh as an example.

He is the university man with the quality Machiavelli describes as "a happy shrewdness"—the natural-born politician with university training. An organization man, he is committed to the *status quo;* a successful attorney and an educated man, he acts usually according to standards and ideals fixed by his law-abiding parents and the example of successful men.

TOM COLE

Servant of the Lord

➤➤➤➤➤➤➤➤➤➤➤➤➤➤➤➤➤➤➤➤➤➤➤➤➤➤➤««-«««-«««-«««-«««-«««-«««-«««-«««-«««-«««-«««-«««-

TURGENEV once said that love and politics were the most interesting things in life. Tom Cole, however, who has been a division leader for more than forty years, would rank religion far above politics, to say nothing of love. He is a successful politician, too, for he has not lost his division once in all this time, and in April, 1932, he gave Butler fewer than ten votes in his fight against Senator Davis; and his own election to the ward committee was so well in hand that he received 196 votes, his partner 195, and there were no opponents with more than ten votes. He carried his division against Roosevelt and the great depression in 1933 and 1934. The most bitter fight of his career, however, was in 1928—all of his people are wet, and most of them are Roman Catholics—when he won for Hoover by a margin of 33.

"My father was neither a minister nor a politician; no one but myself. It was the biggest mistake of my life that I ever entered politics. . . . I can think of three different cases of men that I have brought back to the church, and today one of them is my partner on the ward committee. Fourteen years ago this man was low down through drink. My attention was called to him through his wife being sick. He had a wonderful wife and three children. His wife had tuberculosis. He came to me for help and I sat up with her seven nights in order to give him rest. You don't find many people that will go that far. He had no means or nothing. On her dying bed this woman asked me, 'Mr. Cole, will you promise me that my children will never be separated—that Henry will never put them in a home?' I told her that was a hard task, but I would promise her this—'If I can keep them together I'll endeavor to do so.' After she died I got him a position with the city and helped him along. I took him over to the Catholic church, which is not my faith, but that does not matter to me. I know a Sister of Charity and I talked with her, and then I took him over to the priest. I followed him up and he is attending to his church duties.

"I have worked with ministers and priests in hundreds of cases. They come to me, too. Different clergymen refer men to me. I can take you down to my district now and show you Catholic men that came to me and told me the priest sent them. While I am a politician, I do a lot of church work, too. When I am right with my blessed Christ I can preach and do preach. I sang in choirs for twenty years. I have been superintendent of Sunday Schools for longer than that. I am one out of a thousand in politics."

I then asked if he found it difficult to connect religion with politics. "That is where you make a mistake," he answered. "As a religious man it is my duty to pick up the poor prostitute and help her the best you can, not to prosecute her. Our Lord—you know what he done. The woman with the seven husbands—he converted her at the well. Of course there are a thousand things that you wouldn't dare do. For instance, a man is locked up for bootlegging, and gives the long arm, as we call it—stealing. A woman came to me three nights ago and said her man was arrested. I said, 'What's the trouble?' She said 'Nothing.' Of course, you know, it is always nothing. I went to the station house, and here it was high-way robbery, theft, and enough things to send him away for twenty years. The wife was there so I had to use judgment. I said, 'I'll look into it.' I just simply walked out the door and didn't take part in it one way or another."

Mr. Cole is small of stature like Zacchaeus, to whom he proudly refers. He is a spare little man like another Pennsylvanian of national note, only Mr. Cole has warm, expressive eyes and a big dropping mustache that is parted by the cigar held between his teeth. He is sixty-three years old. He got an early start in politics because his friendly smile and genial nature attracted the attention of an ambitious politician, who asked Mr. Cole to make a fight in the division as a Vare delegate to the state convention. He won and the next year he was elected to the ward committee. Since then he has had four partners on the committee: (1) a business man who was a wholesale butcher; (2) an internal revenue collector: (3) a stock and bond broker; (4) the present one, who is a general laborer. As the class of people in the division has changed in the forty years, so have the representatives on the party committee. Mr. Cole is the same man, but the burden of his work, especially poor relief and station-house matters, has increased so much that "politics just isn't the same!" In spite of his attitude toward certain law violations he serves his people day and night. On one particular day in May, I learned that nineteen constituents had come to him during the preceding twenty-four hours for either (*a*) something to eat, (*b*) medical help, or (*c*) magistrate hearings.

Mr. Cole could barely write his own name when he was thirteen years old. Later he bought some books and educated himself. "If I didn't understand anything I always went and asked someone who could teach me." He said, with regard to his business career, "For the first eighteen years in politics I was in business for myself—in the wholesale fruit and produce business. Finally I got this job at City Hall, where I have been ever since. I could not manage both."

In the April primary in 1932 nineteen or twenty men asked Mr. Cole for work at the polls. "I didn't need them but they had no money. I paid them $67 out of my own pocket, and $30 was given to us by the ward leader to run the division. When I left the polling place that night I had ten cents and a car token and I am still obligated.

"Wherever there is a kid I always pat him on the head or shoulder—from a baby up. People say, 'If you smack my baby on the cheek and love it, you get my vote.'"

The highwater marks of Mr. Cole's political experiences, however, are not the totals of material votes (though he does not neglect them), but his opportunities to help people and, if not to bring them to the fold, at least to give them a sermon, for he considers himself

105

an emissary of God as well as of Vare. "I have had many blessings and many reverses and from the fact of this point I have learned that a man in political life has a wonderful opportunity to serve his God. I have had many cases of bringing daughters and boys from jail that has made a mistake, and I have saw the mothers throw their arms around their children and I saw the tears flow from many eyes. I always said something to help them and to carry out the will of God. At that time when the heart is most susceptible for both the mother and child—so I have always said, 'Well, Mommy and daughter, I'm glad you are home!' I always tell them just three things: '(1) Think of what you was; (2) think of what you are today; and (3) think of what you can become tomorrow if you accept the advice of a mother and look to the Lord.' I leave it at that."

TIMOTHY FLANAHAN

Neighbor

>>>->>>->>>->>>->>>->>>->>>->>>->>>->>>><<<-<<<-<<<-<<<-<<<-<<<-<<<-<<<-<<<-<<<-<<<-<<<-

I WENT to see Tim at his house. He is a big Irishman, at least six feet tall, and well built. His skin is red and his thick black hair is carefully brushed. He has an Irish twang to his speech, and a sparkle in his eyes. Hefty shoulders, thick neck, square jaw—the ensemble belong to one who has come up, but not so far up that he would not stand and deliver handsomely in a rough and tumble fight. He is a two-fisted politician even though his ward is one of the three most independent ones in Philadelphia. Tim's division is organization, however.

I asked him if I might smoke. He answered, "Certainly; it is a poor politician who will not permit anyone to do anything in his house outside of spitting on the ceiling.

"I worked around the polls in the Twenty-fifth Ward when I was twenty-two years old. Billy Campbell and my mother lived together as children. Every fellow on Richmond learned politics from Billy Campbell. When I moved into the XYZ Ward I didn't bother about it until Billy Campbell got me to plug for him. I was here about a year before I got started—got elected to the committee, and have been here ever since.

107

"I have been living in this division over seventeen years. Since we first came into it it has been made into about five different divisions. Being up here as an old residenter the people come to the polls and say, 'How long have I been living here, Tim?' I haven't lived in this house all the time. I first came to the pike. There were no houses here then. This was all farm. I seen this neighborhood grow from a farm.

"When I first came, I was running a laundry route and I got acquainted that way, too. Mr. Fisher was the committeeman, just retired. I went out and took his place, and he stayed out until two years ago and then I insisted that he come back with me.

"When I first came I got active in all the different civic activities. We needed schools, street paving, street lights, and fixing of some embankments. My little girl was one of the ones chosen to raise the flag on the Andrew Jackson school when it was built—opened in 1921. It was an extraordinary honor. Many people didn't know how or why she was picked when she was at the time attending parochial school. However, it was satisfactory to everyone. At that time I was an officer of the improvement association. All the streets needed improvements."

I asked Tim where he comes in contact with his people—where he meets them.

"Right here," he responded. "My door is never locked, day or night. I have something here that not many of the men have—an extension on my telephone that reaches right to my bed—it is about thirty feet long. But I seen myself transact business when I was lying with pneumonia. I got up and went to the station house, against the orders of the doctor. When I got there the magistrate said, 'What's the matter with you, Tim?' I told him I had gotten up out of my sick-bed. He said, 'You're crazy! Why didn't you get in touch with me over the phone?' 'No,' I said, 'When I do anything, I like to see it is properly done.' I wasn't thinking of myself or even of my family, but of the people who elected me to serve them. I feel if the people feel I'm good enough to represent them in the division, then I should be at their service just the same. That is the way I look at it.

"People are coming here all the time, and if I'm not here, my wife serves them just as well as I do. There's never a day but someone comes in. I think she would be lost if someone didn't come in. People say they don't know how she can stand it, but she says she would think we were friendless if there wasn't someone coming in." He went and called his wife. "She is doing something; she is like that—always doing, doing. My wife would rather be around here than go to the movies. I have been married eighteen years."

Mrs. Flanahan came in, and I gave her an idea of what I was asking her husband. She is thick set—not comely but substantial looking and adequate.

"Well," she said, "We have plenty to do between us. I do anything, but I won't stand at the polls. There are too many men around, and, well—he doesn't need me."

"There is always one person a day," Tim broke in, "And sometimes three or four come in. Some of the things I do are this kind. One man came over and told me that he wanted to take his tree down, but he wasn't allowed to unless he was going to put up another one. He asked me to get him a permit, for he had gone for one before but it had not been granted. We got it for him, and when he was filling it out he came over again, and asked what reason he should put down. I told him to say that the pavement was too narrow. He did, and we got the permit granted for him.

"A woman wanted a death certificate to get her husband's insurance. A man called up the other day and said that his wife was living in another division. He wanted to know where his wife voted, for if she was voting from her mother's house he would have her arrested. But we wouldn't have anything to do with that. We said, 'In a couple of weeks you will be back with your wife, and then we would be the worst people alive. The best thing you can do is to go back with your wife.'"

I then asked them about a reputedly successful committeeman in the ward who had never gone to school. Flanahan exclaimed, "I don't want to criticize, but God forbid that I would serve the people in the same way he serves them!" "Yes," his wife put in, "he serves them if they pay him!"

Tim continued. "No one can say that I ever took one penny off them. I don't know how many complaints have come right here where Mautz charged at least a dollar car fare. He will say, 'I have to have car fare.' People sometimes have given him $5.00 to pay a bill that was $3.00 and something, and he had not returned anything—that was his car fare! Charlie Knight done everything for Mautz. Mautz came up to Charlie's office and said he was 100 per cent for him and against Hand [the ward leader], and all that sort of thing. Charlie said, 'All right—I'll take you at your word.' He put coal in Mautz's cellar for him, food on his table, and got him a job. I don't know what he didn't do for him. He had the appointment in writing from the banking department, and he used that with Harden and Hank Stevens [another leader] to be put in the organization after Charlie had gone to all that trouble for him. When I start to do that kind of stuff, and take money for favors, I hope they lick me! Mautz helps the people just before election. If he isn't out there on the corner where he bums, he's inside, playing poker. I've known his wife for years. He has never done a day's work in his life, except sell pop corn and hot dogs at the fights. He has gambled all his life. He is a hard worker for the dollars. He collects from everyone he does anything for. But it is his division, and it's immaterial to me how he runs it!'' (This feeling of righteous indignation and jealousy is often present when one mentions the name of an especially successful fellow-politician.)

I asked Tim if there were any Jews in his division. He said there were only about twelve Jewish families. "About a quarter of the people in my division are Catholics. I was accused on election day—and if it had not been election day, somebody would have been in the hospital, either he or me!—of being a bigot—and God forbid that I will ever be that! A man who has been my partner was a thirty-second degree Mason, and he worked all day in the polls with me. My very best friend in the division today is a young fellow who lives around the corner. He is a minister and his parents come around here often. He never passes here unless he stops in and says, 'Hello, Tim—I just wanted to stop in and say "how are you?"' There's a picture there—[he pointed to a picture of the Sacred Heart which was hanging over his desk] My wife can tell you about it better.'' Mrs. Flanahan then told me that a non-Catholic friend of hers had picked out that picture and frame and sent it to her, saying that, if Mrs. Flanahan died first, she wanted the picture back. This friend, though not a Catholic, also asked that, if she should die first, she be given candles.

And Tim said, "No, I'm not ashamed of what I am and no man should be ashamed of what he is. That is why I hang that picture there.

"I never needed money in this division," Tim continued. "I would spend maybe a couple of dollars out of my own pocket. We don't even hand out a thing on election day. We don't even give cigars. I think it is cheap politics to try to buy a man's vote, and think that is trying to buy it. I just feel the same as if I was going around myself to vote, and some politician would try to hand me a cigar or something. I would say, 'What is this—a vote for a cigar?' It was the same condition last election when they were working for Sam Harrison. They had a lot of boxes of matches with his picture on them, and they were handing them out. The people said, 'What are you trying to do—buy my vote with a match?'''

Then Tim began talking about a friend of his, a magistrate, who had been put in jail. "Fenton was

112

unopposed," he said. "He was the victim of his friends higher up in the party. They made a convict out of him. If he had listened to me he would never have been in jail. I told him not to handle some of the fellows he handled. I always liked Fenton and I helped him when he needed a friend. He was the best leader this ward ever had. I don't say he is an ex-convict, but a victim of his friends. We argued, but still I always liked him; we never lost our friendship. When he was elected magistrate he was elected by such majorities which licked the Harden-Stevens section. He said to me, 'Tim, Harden and those fellows are coming over with us.'

"'Well,' I said, 'You're older than I am, but I don't like it. The day you take them in you are making an awful mistake; if I were you, I wouldn't do it.'

"Fenton said, 'Well, if we take them in, it may strengthen us—Maybe it will help.'

"The day that he told me they had come over and that he had accepted them, I put my hand out and said, 'Let me shake your hand as a friend, but from now on you are a dead issue.' That was in 1924–1926. Fenton was the leader for about eight years. He had more jobs than anybody else. He was a man who wouldn't take 'No' from Ed Vare, Kendrick, or any Director. He would go right up to them and take his man in with him. It was funny to listen to him. I heard him go into the Mayor once—he was sincere but he was abrupt—he would say, 'You fathead, you pork-head, you pineapple—I have to have this job, and I won't leave until I have it!' He had fifty jobs on the subway alone. Blumstein [another committeeman] was an inspector on the subway. Somebody else made out the reports and he would sign them to do the best he could. Dick Gorham, who only kept a hot-dog stand or something of that sort, was an inspector too. After Fenton lost we all lost our jobs. I always liked him and still do like him."

Not long ago, Tim was double-crossed by a political associate who circulated the following letter about him:

Is your committeeman a Real Friend to You? Your present Republican Committeeman who is asking you to re-elect him, claims to be a real friend to his constituents. Before election-time a number of property-holders are asked to sign petitions for a reduction in assessments. But it proves to be only a dud—a pre-election trick.

He does not tell you that he keeps down his own assessment. His property is assessed at $2,600. Compare this with yours. He, being a committeeman, ask him why he cannot do as much for you.

By the way, this same committeeman now supports Governor Pinchot and his party in Philadelphia. He owes his appointment on the boxing commission also in the State Labor Bureau, to the Pinchot organization.

Your vote is respectfully solicited for

This was the culmination of various hints of treason, Tim said, and he reflected, "There is not the double-crossing in the South Philadelphia districts that there is up here. Down there they stick together." Mrs. Flanahan went on to say that there was a woman down the street who had seen Summers "going in and out here for all that time—they called him Tim's shadow;

114

and when she got that letter she said, 'What did that bird want that he didn't get?'" Mrs. Flanahan went on to explain the accusations, none of which were true she said, and concluded by saying, "Well, it is a good thing that he didn't know anything bad about Tim; that is all he knew." And she derived great satisfaction from the knowledge she had that "lots of people got those letters and wouldn't read such trash." One person said, "If I had known his address I would have put a note on the back of it and sent it right back to him!"

Tim said that Billy Campbell, the big political leader of a neighboring section of Philadelphia, had talked with him about Summers, among other things. Billy knows thousands of people, and knew Summers only slightly, but he had answered, "That's not a surprise to you, is it?" Tim had answered, "Yes, it is, in a way, knowing that the man has been sitting around my home for three years." "Well," said Billy, "the Summers boys came from up the state in 1900, and for the first couple of years I did lots of favors for them; but in 1904 they double-crossed me and Boies Penrose who was my friend—so what can you expect?" That was going back a good many years, but Billy's memory was good.

Speaking of Billy Campbell, I asked Tim what he thought of this leader—what made him a great leader?

"Why is Billy Campbell a great leader?" he said. "His success is the same as I attribute mine to. He knows his people by the first name; has an open door and office down there that anybody can go to. You don't have to go to an office boy and give him your name and if he doesn't like your name he is busy or he isn't in. You can look in his office and see whether he is in or not. He is there all the time to serve them. He knows his people all the time—not only on election day. Naturally, he would get jobs, more so than a committeeman, being ward leader and having power out here and all his different offices that he has held. He is not an educated man. He didn't even graduate from grammar school. He is a self-made man. His first job in politics paid $900 a year. I could tell you every job he has held practically. I am in his office every day. Most of those fellows who are around his office are from out here— fellows with whom I was born and raised. Billy is not a great publicity man. You know, it's funny. You can go to Billy's office and the phone will ring, and you never hear him say, 'This is Register of Wills Campbell'—just, 'This is Billy Campbell.' Just plain Billy Campbell. If a woman comes in, it is, 'Hello, Mary'—not 'Mrs.'

"He used to be able to tell you pretty nearly all the people in Richmond" [the name of his section of the city]. Mrs. Flanahan broke in, "Could he pronounce the names now? They are all Polish now!" Tim continued, "Campbell is a fine fellow. He has a shrewd brain. He can see things in advance of the political game. What other leader would have the nerve to come out and fight for the northeast district and council when they tried to make all kinds of offers to take out Daly? [Daly is a member of council whom the organization men were trying to replace with a Vare man.] The big fellows said, 'We'll concede you anything if you take out Daly.' But Campbell said, 'He doesn't go out.' What other man would have done it? Look at the number of jobholders he was jeopardizing by that! He would have lost the jobs in the county offices; he would have no control of City Treasurer, or Clerk of Quarter Sessions. This is what it would have been. Eleventh and Chestnut [party headquarters] would have brought pressure on, say, the County Commissioner's office to discharge Billy's men. In spite of that, Campbell wouldn't withdraw Daly. They wouldn't order those discharges now because of his support in the coming elections. Also, there are lots of bills that come before council that need a certain number of votes—for instance, to pass a bill over the mayor's veto, there must be a two-thirds majority. Well, if Vare wanted something like that passed, he would need Billy's support. He has a number of votes that always go along with him."

Tim, reflecting then on the big men with fat pocketbooks, still in politics, said, "If I had the money that Bill Johnson has got, I would forget politics and everything else. But it is a profit to them in their business. [Johnson is a contractor.] None of those big fellows are in politics for their health. There is a fascination to them in a financial way."

I asked Tim and his wife if they would encourage their son, a fine, big fellow who had been in and out while we were talking, to go into politics. They both answered very emphatically "Absolutely no." Tim said, "Now that I am in it, I wouldn't like to be beaten, but if I had it to do over again, I should never go into it again. I fully appreciate the honor, but still I wouldn't go into it if I weren't already in it. But I've just heard a story going around the corner at Fifth and Texas Street, and

117

a man told me that if anybody would say anything about me there, they would probably be ringing for the wagon or the ambulance.''

Tim told me then something about his social-service activities as a division leader. ''My partner and I have gone through the division on Saturdays sometimes. My partner goes through one part of the division and my youngster goes through the other part. They go from door to door to different ones who have promised such things as bread, milk, sugar, canned vegetables. We make up fourteen baskets which are given to fourteen different families who are out of employment. We have given out about 225 baskets in less than six months. I get the ones to pledge, and Mr. Fisher gets them in the other part. This is limited to the division alone. Every Saturday after dark, so that no one will know that anyone else is getting it, we distribute them to worthy cases in the division. Besides that, every once in a while, we give a half-ton of coal here and there. We pay for that ourselves. I am a Notary Public, and in four years time I sit here and don't clear my expenses on Notary for people in the division. Sure, a person comes in from the division and I know that fifty cents means a lot to them, and I wouldn't think of taking that fifty cents. Last November I personally put on three hundred seals in this ward on petitions to try to have assessments reduced, and I didn't receive one cent for a notary seal. Neither would I accept a cent. I brought the petitions up myself from the Hall, put the seals on, and filed them in City Hall. In City Hall one of the real-estate assessors remarked, 'Flanahan must have gotten a good pile out of those seals!' But I can say here on a stack of Bibles I didn't receive one cent. I never once took a penny from one person for one service rendered in this division or outside this division. I made that a practice when I went into politics that no one could ever say that I took money for favors.

"In 1919 Ed Vare urged me to take a job as a prohibition agent. I told him I was raising children and that I needed work, but no one would be able to point to any of my children and say their father was a prohibition agent and a grafter. Vare said, 'Flanahan, you don't have to be a grafter.' I said, 'No? No one can say that I try to induce a man to break the law and shake him down afterwards!' Vare said, 'Well, I don't think you would make a very good prohibition agent.' A fellow came to me then and said, 'I hear you turned down a job as prohibition agent; will you help me get it?' I said, 'If you want a rat's job, you can have it as far as I am concerned!' I got the job for him. He made a lot of money, but today he hasn't a cent. He ran around—high life and everything else. It was ill-gotten money, and it went."

Tim keeps a scrapbook in which are a dozen newspaper clippings and as many letters referring to him in terms of high praise. Here are a few of them.

DEAR MR. FLANAHAN,

Just a few kind words of thanks to you for being so good to me in time of my need and the children as through your helping hand toward me, the workers up on Broad Street are wonderful. They do treat you with kindness and give with a good heart, and everything is well thanked for. I hope you

119

are up and around soon so you can be able to attend to your business real soon. It is no fun being sick and have so much to think of also. Well, I said a prayer for you and your dear family last evening so I hope the dear Lord will reward you and all your dear friends for being good to the poor families of today. The boy is much better now. I am well pleased over it as I was worried sick about him. Well I will close now. I remain, . . .

("That lady had a home here in the neighborhood but due to the depression they became destitute. She was forced to sell her home and all her furniture. She doesn't live in the division, but she came to me to see if I could help her for some little thing for her children. My wife came in and saw her and said, 'Is that the heaviest clothing you have?' She said, 'I am not interested for myself, but I am interested for my children.' We succeeded in getting her clothes and some for the children, and some food. Also one youngster was very ill. We sent a doctor and immediately he recommended an operation. We sent him to a Jewish hospital. Through our friendship the doctor performed the operation free and also the services of the Jewish Hospital were rendered free of charge.")

I came out O.K., Tim. Renshaw asked me how many children I had. I did not expect much only having *one* child, but he gave me a slip for $4 worth of goods. Thanks. Say, Tim, if it is possible when they get that employment agency up town, would you try to get me in the office or any kind of job. Of course, if you can't get me a job inside, I would be glad to take the pick and shovel if I had to. Hoping you will do the best you can for me. Thanks for the basket.

TIMOTHY FLANAHAN

And here is a newspaper clipping concerning Tim.

CLUB MEMBER GIVEN IMPORTANT POST

Once again has one of our fellow members, and of course one of our parishioners, been honored by high public recognition. We refer in this particular instance to Timothy H. Flanahan (our 'Tim') whose recent appointment to the State Athletic Commission is an honor sufficiently bright to allow the rest of us to bask in its reflected glory.

Flanahan is one of the few committeemen that I know who keeps a record of the vote cast in his division, and sample ballots for years back. Even in a fight he wins by more than two hundred votes.* As a ward politician he is good—he knows it, and so does his wife—and what is more fortunate, an overwhelming majority of the people in his division agree with him in his personal estimate of himself.

* Or he did until 1933 and 1934, when he was barely defeated "not by a politician but by the depression and the President of the United States."

SAM TERNBERG

Ward Heeler

ANOTHER of Philadelphia's successful division leaders is Sam Ternberg. I was talking one day to several committeemen from Ternberg's ward (which happens to be one of the largest and most recently settled in the city). I said to one of the experienced politicians in the group, to whom I had previously given a fine cigar, that the one quality that made for success in politics was energy rather than brains or anything else. Much to my surprise he entirely agreed with me, and added, "Take Ternberg, for example. He is as big as an elephant, and quite dumb. He can neither read nor write, but he is about the best committeeman in the ward. He is always working, always meeting people, and he is out where the people can see him."

Ternberg had been pointed out to me before as I had talked to his comrades in City Hall, and the next time I saw him I spoke to him and told him that I wanted to call at his home for an interview. When I arrived at his house, he was at a neighbor's (where there were six "votes"), but his wife went and got him at once. He is a heavy middle-aged man of medium height, with a very florid face and a sloping forehead. His friends call him an Irish-Jew—he is Jewish himself, but he married a Catholic. He is partially bald, and has coarse features; he looks like a football player or an iceman a little past his prime, and seems to possess plenty of physical vigor. He was pleased to see me, and cordially greeted me, as he had on several occasions before, with the salutation, "Hello, stranger!"

I told him that I had heard that he was one of the most successful of the many committeemen in his ward, and that I wanted to write about him in my book. He was pleased at the idea, although he had seemed heretofore unconscious of his own importance. I began by saying, "Suppose you had a son eighteen years old that was going to devote himself exclusively to politics, and that the doctor had told you that you would die before he had reached his twenty-first birthday, and that you wanted to tell him all you knew about politics so that he might become a successful politician within the shortest possible time. What would you tell him?" Ternberg appeared to be following my words with solemn comprehension. When I had stopped talking, he looked a bit perplexed; then he said, "So you think your son is going to die?"

I then tried another approach. I asked him to tell me how he got the people in his division to vote the way he wanted them to on election day. This question he understood. He then settled back in his chair, and this is what he told me:

"I see all my voters, keep good friends with them, and do them favors. [There are more than seven hundred in his division.] As soon as new people move into my division, I call on them, and tell them who I am—the

123

organization man. There's where I was just now. There were six votes in that house. I see the people not once a year, but every day in the week. I always have a good word for them every time I see them. I smile and bid them the top of the day. The only way to succeed in politics is to get out and work for the people. [Some of Ternberg's acquaintances accuse him of using the "crying towel"—"vote for my ticket so I can keep my job at City Hall."] You must get acquainted with them. My father was in politics before me. He learned me politics. He showed me what politics was. In this game you got to mix in with all your people. If your people know you so good, you can call them by their first name. I get out of bed at three and four in the morning to help a person in trouble. I don't get back until seven or eight o'clock, and then go to the police station to speak to the magistrate, when my person comes up for a hearing. It's all in the game of politics—if you don't serve your people, they won't vote for you. I got out of bed more than once to help a fellow and I never turned a man down in my life yet.

"Of course, I always heard politics talked at home, and when I came up in this ward I was out of work. I went into politics for a ten-dollar note. I was paid this to help around the polls on election day. A year later I had made enough friends so that I got elected to the ward committee. The other committeeman needed someone to help him. He knew me and he liked the way I worked. He backed me at my first election, eleven years ago, and since then I have been able to stand on my own feet, although my partner, who is an attorney, and I

124

always work together. Now I guess I am the one who controls the division. I have never lost it in an election yet.

"In the evening I often loaf at a saloon at Fifth and X Streets, where I meet some of my people. Plenty call me at City Hall. [He is one of the men in charge of the prisoners that are taken from the cell rooms to the courts in the same building.] Other people call at my house too. If I am not there, my wife always knows where I am. Sometimes I am with a group of men playing pinochle. There is an average of three or four people a day that come to me for favors. These favors usually are police-station matters, or helping some person get a job."

His wife interrupted at this point and said, "He is a charity committeeman, a charity politician. We can't save a nickel around here, but we use all our money in helping other people. Now in this depression we are so poor that we had to give up the telephone."

He went on to say, "I know all the magistrates, and, if a case comes up before a magistrate, I can handle that myself; or if I need to see a city councilman, I can do that. But if there is a question that involves the Mayor, I get our ward leader to take care of that for me. I usually go to the ward leader in case something must be done that requires the cooperation of department heads or bureau chiefs. Of course it all depends upon whether I know these men or not. Men I know I talk to, and those that I don't know I get the leader to talk to for me. He knows them all. They will listen to him where they wouldn't pay any attention to me.

125

"This is the sort of favors I do—an alley may be dark and the people living there may want a light. I report this to the bureau of lighting. I sometimes see the Highway Commissioner in order to get jobs for voters, or in case the construction work on a street is not done properly. I see the street-cleaning department about keeping the streets in my neighborhood clean. If the people in my division make a complaint I see what can be done about it. Sometimes a policeman in my division is given a beat way downtown, and I get him switched up in his own neighborhood. The members of a party are like one big family—we all do things for each other."

Mr. Ternberg's wife interrupted again to say that her husband is always on the go. "He can't stay still; he snores a lot at night, and sometimes goes to sleep sitting in a chair after supper. He bummed school; he can't read or write so good."

This being unable to read has its drawbacks even in the case of the willing Ternberg. At one primary election a worker for the opposition deftly exchanged his specially marked sample ballots for those that Ternberg was giving out to the voter. (In this ward the voter marks his own ballot—he is not "assisted.") But when the ward leader visited Ternberg's division and asked for a sample ballot the matter was straightened out.

He is often to be found on the corner where the trolley stops. He helps the women off the car with their baskets of provisions, and mothers with their babies. He not only helps them to the street, but in special cases he accompanies the woman to her door. He does it without condescension. He suggests that he is the people's servant and that they have a right to expect any sort of real service from him. He is not always the soul of tact, however; I observed him one primary election night and saw him roughly jump before two young women who tried to enter the polling place a few minutes after closing. And if the argument runs against him in a close-up political fight he is certain to swing his ham-like fist at the center of the opposition.

Ternberg said that he saw his ward leader every day in the week, and also on Sunday. "He is my best friend," he said, "and he is a real leader. If he would tell me to go to hell, I would go. I go to see him even when I have no favors to ask, merely because I like to see him, and I do not want him to forget."

Mrs. Ternberg spoke up again and said, "A politician's life is all right when you have a job, but when you lose your job, it's bad. [He was once employed on a subway and he would get a fellow employee to look after his work while he sold pop and hot dogs at a ball park.] Then you must serve the people and get nothing for it. Another thing that is bad is that we can never leave this place—never move to any other section. This house needs a lot of repairs, but we must stay, because a politician must live where his friends are. Otherwise he must start all over again. His friends in the division are his political capital."

Ternberg watched me write as he talked. "You can write awfully fast. I bet you could make a hundred dollars a week writing." When the interview was nearly over he asked me to read what he had told me. I did.

He looked very happy and smiled at his wife. She seemed pleased, too. When I left he told me that he wanted to be sure that I had his name spelled right, and said that if I ever got arrested he would help me, too

GEORGE KENDALL

Gentleman

>>>>>>>>>>>>>>>>>>>>>>>>>>>>>>>>>>>>>>><<<<<<<<<<<<<<<<<<<<<<<<<<<<

GEORGE KENDALL always strikes me as being too gentle to be a full-fledged follower of Vare. He might have been a Y. M. C. A. secretary or a teacher in a private school. He is courteous, mild mannered, and friendly; he is a handsome man, of average height, well built, with a patrician face and a head of fine, steel-gray hair with a wave in it. He wears a freshly pressed gray or blue suit with tie to match. He is genial but not effusive. He is amiable and likes to talk politics—national, state, or the more personal sort that belongs to the life in his district. He is eloquent rather than penetrating—a lawyer that knows so much that he cannot easily learn more. He is fairly well satisfied with himself—no inferiority complexes ruffle him.

Another division leader, one of these dark-eyed, short, thick-set fellows, with heavy red cheeks and a chin and a half, told me about George Kendall. "He is the man you want to meet, professor. He is a lawyer and he can tell you all about politics so it will look nice in your book." (However, months later I was again talking to this same bruiser and several other ward committeemen in the corridor on the sixth floor of City Hall. Kendall's name was mentioned in connection with an important case in his ward. These men—all friendly to him—agreed that they would never take Kendall as their attorney in a situation like this. I asked why. "He hain't got the guts—he won't do what's got to be done to win a hard case. He is a nice fellow but it takes something else to save your man in some of these courts.") Later this same friendly division leader introduced me to George. He was pleasant and invited me over to his office. He seemed mildly interested in the idea that someone was writing a book on his organization.

A few days later I called. He offered me a chair, presented a cigar which he urged me to take, and started to give me typical textbook information on the national committee and other general political subjects, including a personal estimate of the attributes of the Mayor and the ward leaders of Philadelphia. It was thirty minutes before we got to Mr. Kendall's first-hand experience in the game of hopes and sorrows.

He got started in politics shortly after he cast his first vote. His natural charm had won him many friends—he is always a pleasant person to meet—and he lived then and now in a newly developed part of the city. He took a hand in elections, and campaigned for the organization ticket. As a young attorney he did many favors for the people in his neighborhood without presenting a bill. He is of a generous disposition, and, besides, he was making new friends, and friends are capital either in politics or law. At the end of six years he was elected to the party committee—a division leader. For fourteen years he has been an enthusiastic and loyal party committeeman.

130

Mr. Kendall usually campaigns in a district wider than his own in state and national campaigns. In the 1930 gubernatorial primary he was one of a select group of organization men that traveled over the state in automobiles. He made speeches, and with his companions he saw contact men, and met the county chairmen in twenty-nine of the sixty-seven counties of the state.

He also writes letters to the press (an unheard-of thing among division leaders). One letter that he showed me was more than four hundred words long. It was on the ideals of George Washington and the regrettable state of political indifference on the part of our young people today. In this letter he quoted George Washington's farewell address and a recent speech of former Senator Pepper. Another unusual thing is his scrapbooks filled with pertinent newspaper clippings. Again I thought, he is the teacher type—division leaders very rarely keep scrapbooks, and still more rarely elaborate ones filled with such complete data on politics.

The goal nearest his heart is to be endorsed by the organization for the state legislature. Clay never wanted to be President more than Kendall wants to be an assemblyman. But I am afraid he will never go. He is too genuinely friendly and too mild mannered. The men with more grit and stubbornness get the endorsements. When the new district attorney took office George had the promise of a place under him. But when his list of the new assistant district attorneys was given out George's name was not on it. His friends were more sorry than surprised. It merely meant that the place had been given to the favorite of a more determined ward leader than Kendall has. Sometimes it pays to be stubborn and to annoy the organization. It may then bribe you with a job to secure peace.

To him a division leader is not a public official, yet he is none the less a person of great power for good or evil in the community in which he lives. The people count heavily upon him and it behooves him to serve them well. He feels that it is second nature for committeemen to be kind and helpful. The real committeeman will serve people twenty-four hours a day. Kendall sometimes expresses his philosophy of life and politics by quoting a bit of the writings of Edgar Guest. "He is not the richest who out of life takes only gold. Richer far are they who serve the young and old. He is the richest who can say I have neighbored down the way."

The ward in which Kendall lives is so big that for party administrative purposes it is divided into sections. Before the fall primary I attended one of the sectional meetings, at which sixty-five committeemen were present. I recognized seven of them as men I had often talked to at City Hall. They gave me a cordial greeting and so did Mr. Kendall. He also introduced me to some of the other division leaders. The meeting began at 8:30 o'clock, lasted until after ten, and Mr. Kendall most ably served as chairman. He was easily the most distinguished-looking man present, not excepting the candidate for council and the leader of the ward. He was also the best speaker.

After a few introductory remarks, he called on an old-time division leader. This speaker made a brief speech

132

extolling Frank Henley, the new organization candidate for city council. "Frank Henley," he said, "is not high-hat, as some of you think he is. He is a real fellow, he likes rum and plays poker. [Applause.] This is our one opportunity to have representation in council. You must get your people to register." (Emphasis was placed on the word "your." This ward is one of the few independent wards of the city—many of the voters take pride in voting for nonorganization candidates—therefore the committeemen must use discretion in getting only the loyal to register. One of the committeemen here told me that he couldn't win his division if more than two hundred people voted in it. The organization loyalists always vote—the independent ones are never asked to, but sometimes they vote anyway. The problem of these politicians is to appear to be interested in having everyone exercise his right to franchise, but actually to see that only the faithful do. This division leader explained that on registration day he might unexpectedly meet an independent who would say, "Today is registration day—I must register." He would answer, "Oh, there are two other days, why bother?" If the question comes up on the morning of the third day he will say, "Oh, it's early yet—there is plenty of time—you know you can register at night.")

The speaker then paid a tribute to the ward leader: "He battled with the organization downtown to put Frank Henley over. It is up to us to make him win—otherwise our leader will be a poor fish in Philadelphia. The leader supported you—he is now entitled to your support." And the burden of the remarks of the ward leader and other speakers was in substance the message of the committeeman whom I have quoted.

On another occasion I attended a meeting of both independent and organization leaders and candidates in the same ward. There were seventeen candidates for the Republican nomination from this district to council. The purpose of the meeting was to eliminate sixteen in order actually to nominate and elect one. Each of the sixteen independent candidates approved of the idea in principle, but he would not budge an inch, said that he personally was in the hands of his friends, and would do whatever they asked him to. Frank Henley was at another meeting but his proxy—George Kendall—spoke for him. Mr. Kendall spoke with ease and charm, and, although he probably did no more than the candidates that spoke, in changing opinions, yet he acquitted both his friend and himself well.

He described Mr. Henley as a successful business man, a person of integrity and "one who will bring to you the united support of the organization, which means twelve thousand votes at the start." Someone sought to embarrass him with, "Will Mr. Henley withdraw if the rest of the candidates do?" Mr. Kendall paused a moment, looked at the interrogator and replied, "Mr. Henley is in the same position that you gentlemen are in. He is in the hands of his friends."

The candidate himself came a few minutes later and was called upon to address the group. He is short, thick set, with a florid complexion and bushy grey hair reminiscent of the elder La Follette. He walks quickly— with a strutting step like a pouter pigeon's. He does not look like an organization man and I had to remind myself that this was the most independent of all the wards. The self-complacency in his appearance was not so evident in his speaking. He was very ineffective in this role, and, although ward nominations are but little more affected by public speeches than the earth is by the passing of Saturn on its orbit, he probably counteracted much of the good impression his friend had made.

I told Kendall later that hearing him speak for his friend and then hearing the friend speak for himself reminded me that Garfield had once won a nomination to the Presidency by the excellence with which he performed a similar service. Kendall smiled in appreciation, but he said, "Ward politicians are different—it takes something else to win endorsements by the organization here."

Shortly after Christmas I called again to learn more specifically about the services that Kendall gave his people. First of all he made a statement that he particularly wanted me to take down. It follows: "I want it distinctly understood that in all the time that I have been dabbling in politics that I have never been asked to do anything wrong, in the sense that it was criminally wrong, by any member of the Republican organization in Philadelphia, from top to bottom, or by anyone indirectly connected with it."

Questions are not often wholly right or wrong in politics. When a person is in trouble it is often over a legal matter and when he wants help he wants it badly; a politician that might say, "I could help you but it would not be legal, so therefore I won't," would not survive a single election. Mr. Kendall knows this and it causes him anxious moments. He made the foregoing statement to satisfy his pride and because his is an unusually sensitive personality in politics.

Christmas time he and his partner gave thirty-six baskets of provisions to the poorest families in his district. Mr. Kendall delivered these baskets in person. "There are many poor people in my division as well as some wealthy ones. Last night four of the bitterly poor ones stopped at my home. One was a woman seventy-five years of age who is up against it. She has no money and she has two sons in Camden. I agreed to send for her boys and pay her $2.00 a week in the meantime.

"Mr. Hagins came to see if I could get his daughter, a partial paralytic, in a Jewish hospital. She badly needs hospital treatment and I am trying to get her admitted. The man across the way from my home is out of work. He wanted me to buy a big bottle of ink. I didn't need any unknown brand of ink but I bought the bottle just the same. A young chap was there to get me to see the ward leader about having him put back as a clerk in the electrical bureau."

Kendall then opened his file and took out a folder containing between one hundred and two hundred separate typewritten items—all matters relating to his work as attorney and division leader for a period of six months—July-December, 1931. He informed me that his records of services for his people for other six-month periods were as great as this. He pulled several bundles from his file in order to show me. I began to examine them and I was quite convinced of his usefulness to his people. Some he was wary about showing me lest he involve someone else. In one case he helped defend a young man arrested for transporting liquor, and at the hearing the boy alleged that he was hauling for a prominent ward leader in the liquor business. Needless to say I promised not to use any names. Finally George took up the most recent six months' bundle of typewritten notes and carbons of letters, and briefly recounted a number of his most meritorious services. I shall quote several of them here. (The fact that he keeps his records so carefully is another definite indication that he is unique as a politician—most of the ones I know best keep no written notes at all.)

"I organized an improvement group for the purpose of securing a semaphor and signal light in the community in which my division has its boundaries.

"I also represented approximately ten fathers of about twenty children who were charged with malicious mischief, children under sixteen years of age, the acts being petty and mischievous pranks, but destructive of property rights. Through association with the Big Brother Movement we persuaded the authorities to give these lads another chance in view of the fact that they had never been apprehended before for any criminal charge.

"Two weeks ago I represented relatives who were indirectly connected with four young New York youths who had hired an automobile, and who were charged with the larceny of it. But the true facts turned out to be

137

that they had been given permission to drive the car out of the State of New York, but for some unaccountable reason it was not noted on the records of the garage system. These boys had never been arrested before, and were properly discharged.

"I represented one of my constituents in a domestic relations case in Delaware County, which is an adjoining county of Philadelphia. While the matter was generally outside of a committeeman's duties politically, I undertook the matter in view of the distress of the family, the matter involving the custody and maintenance of a small child. The case was happily settled for the best interest of all the parties, particularly the child.

"My partner on the committee and I took up a collection throughout the division as well as some parts of the ward and collected approximately $150, which was expended for coal, bread, clothing, and in one case for the purchase of burialia. They wouldn't bury the woman unless the money was guaranteed. I furnished $25 right here for that, but of course I was repaid that later. The woman was buried in a Jewish cemetery, Mount Sinai, I think.

"I represented one of our constituents before the State Highway Department's Road Bureau at Nineteenth and Oxford, who had been charged with being a hit-and-run driver and failing to render assistance. The facts in the case were that a colored boy had stolen the car and without permission of the owner had taken it out, and within two squares struck another automobile. It turned out that the colored boy had been charged in many other cases for the same reason.

138

"I helped several families who were evicted for failure to pay their rent, in some cases persuading the landlords to hold off until June, and in other cases taking up collections.

"Some of the citizens in the community complained of a smoke nuisance and a petition was filed to abandon this smoke nuisance from a large machine shop. My partner on the ward committee and I removed the evil by arbitration with the owners of the plant.

"We two division leaders represented twenty-seven real-estate owners in filing for a restraining order to prevent the erection of a coal yard in the rear of the twenty-seven houses, and up to now the coal house has not been erected, and the case is still pending. That case necessitated a great deal of work in securing evidence and expert assistance in preparing the case for court. It cost a lot of money. The folks are all very poor. We had to send out photographers to take pictures of the conditions of the place and we had to foot the bill. It cost us more than $100.

"A still just down the street almost blew up the whole block. I represented another woman directly related to these people that had the still. She had about eleven children. She was locked up three or four different times for bootlegging. She was discharged when I told them the case they would have. She would have been turned over to the Board of Charities.

"We had several cases before the Magistrate, involving miscellaneous crimes: malicious mischief, corner lounging—all the boys in the neighborhood were arrested one night—and one particular group of cases involving

139

an automobile trap that had been placed at the intersection of Kereyon and Forty-second Street and no signal light being at the intersection. The general charges against the automobiles were passing each other at the crossing, as well as general speeding. One of these cases was subsequently appealed and the trap broken up.

"A case involving the sale of liquor to a young man who lived in the division, but purchased it in another section of Philadelphia. His parents had warned the saloon-keeper not to sell any liquor to the boy, and the lad had been refused admittance by the saloon-keeper. As a result he went to a neighboring barber shop, got drunk on drinking red wine and went back to the saloon-keeper, and abused him. As a result of this a fight occurred and the boy was sent to the hospital, having been shot through the arm and finger and beaten over the head with a baseball bat. The following day the father wanted to arrest the saloon-keeper on the charge of sale of liquor, but I told him he couldn't do it as he really hadn't sold him any liquor. Subsequently some of the liquor was brought in here which they said had been bought at the saloon-keeper's. They had somebody make a purchase of it paying $10.00 for a ⅝ bottle. The results were that that case had been adjusted before the magistrate by all the parties withdrawing the charges. They were Jewish people. The boy worked for the American Stores Company, wholesale department. He lost that job through liquor business and from there he went through all the wholesale grocery businesses, without getting work. That is why we were interested in the case.

"We always cooperate, and especially during this depression, for the purpose of securing jobs not only politically but anywhere, and did succeed in placing young women and young men in fields entirely removed from politics, such as sales clerk in department stores, book-keepers, stenographers, and in several cases accountants.

"At the Jewish holiday we took care of thirty-two families. We collected all kinds of food, and sent them out in baskets and dispatched them. We were working about two or three weeks. We went to the wharf and bought stuff, and had some given to us.

"For a period of approximately two weeks or three Sundays we represented about seven store-keepers who had been charged with unlawfully keeping their stores open on Sunday or selling merchandise in hours not permitted on Sunday. It appeared in these cases that the sales were of condensed milk, single loaves of bread, bags of salt, and in no case did the sales amount to over a dollar. Some of these sales were within five minutes of the closing time set by the law in Pennsylvania for Sunday closing. Those cases ran over again. The first group were fined $3.50 and costs, and on the following week or first week in June almost every store-keeper in the radius of three or four squares, covering several divisions, was arrested on the same ridiculous charges, and all of them were discharged. It was a different magistrate. The magistrate in the first cases, Magistrate T, had an ax out for us. He is now removed.

"We represented a chicken dealer who was charged with short weight. They went through the neighborhood and arrested several of them. It appeared that he charged 10 cents extra on the pound for the Rabbi's charge for special inspection. There was no charge as to the shortage of weight, but the charge was as to the excessive price, and there is no law that stops a man from fixing the price of his merchandise—he may charge 10 cents or 50 cents. The man was discharged. This spite wasn't Phinny Greens'; he always treated us all right. It seemed to be more just, that Schofield and Belcher made an awful drive on us at that time.

"Through the cooperative assistance of leader X we were able to place a boy in the Dental College at Temple, having him enrolled for the following year.

"We were also successful in securing a job in the playground association, as playground inspector, for a man in my division.

"There was also quite a great deal of service given to families about to be evicted. Here are two examples:

"Family Y, husband and wife and five children, occupy a small two story house in 4900 block in Franklin Street, West Side. They have been helped by the committeemen for a period of three years. In May or June of 1931 they were evicted from one house for non-payment of rent. The husband was engaged as a driver for a milk wagon. He was hurt in some unknown way, but not in the line of his business, and therefore not entitled to compensation. He was unable to secure any employment at all. He was helped by the committeemen and through the local division organization and the Bristol Township Poor Board.

142

"Some people are very poor in our neighborhood; we are doing this kind of work all the time.

"Family Z is a family of five or six children. The husband was a construction carpenter; work got slack and he lost his house through Sheriff's sale. He tried to rent the place and was subsequently evicted for non-payment of rent. He moved into smaller property, was helped by committeemen, and is still living in the division.

"Do I think rich people make as many demands as poor?

"It all depends on the type of wealthy people. You know there are two different kinds of wealthy people—the wealthy person that obeys the law, and the others who for some unaccountable reason disregard the law. Those that fall afoul of the law are the ones that require the help of the committeemen.

"We were asked to place a young woman in Byberry [hospital], which was done after considerable trouble.

"During the summer period there were quite a number of quarrels over children and property rights between the neighbors themselves, and in most of these cases the simple proposition of arbitration was suggested. It generally worked for the best interest of all. Here are some illustrations:

"A doctor complained about the number of children playing in the driveway beside his house. Complaints were made to the police department by the doctor, and a group of children between the ages of eight and fourteen were ordered to be present at the police station.

143

It turned out in this case that the doctor's own son was among the crowd and the matter was adjusted.

"Another group of neighbors got into an argument over dogs that scratched up lawns when they were let loose. Both sides threatened to arrest each other, but were persuaded to look at it in a common-sense manner by both committeemen. Both were right and both were wrong. The dog was subsequently disposed of and the neighbors are now good friends.

"A number of other quarrels arose over scraps between children and the committeemen refused to get into those scraps, but tried to patch up the difficulties.

"Quite a number of domestic relations cases, complaints of husbands and wives, were brought to the committeemen. They wisely refrained from getting mixed up in them. Most were caused by economic depression, and both husband and wife had just causes to complain. Everything was done to amicably arrange their affairs without interfering with their domestic problems.

"The biggest campaign job was to cut down the taxes on fourteen rows of houses in that district. That certainly was a lot of work. Appeals were prepared, a stenographer was hired especially for that work, photographers were taken out to take pictures of the different rows, and assessed valuations of the rows were checked up with other properties in the same ward. We were successful in persuading the Board to reduce, on an average of $500 a house on each row."

Mr. Kendall has a secretary and a comfortable office in one of the most central of office buildings. I would occasionally meet him in a corridor of City Hall and he always greeted me with a friendly smile. His colleagues on the ward committee—I have talked to fifty-seven of them—feel kindly toward him. Great was my surprise therefore, when I learned that, in April, he was defeated for reelection to his party committee. This was City Hall gossip to me before I called on George. The Jews have been steadily increasing in numbers in his division until now it is almost 85 per cent Jewish. A young Jew—vital and aggressive—on the age-old racial issue, beat him by less than fifty votes, and in a poll of more than three hundred. It was generally agreed by his victorious comrades that the Jewish issue did it. (If anyone thinks that race and religion and color do not count in politics, let him study election contests in the smallest unit of all—the divisions.) Kendall is a Gentile and he was beaten as such. His old colleague is a Jew and was reelected. The people partially forgot past services in face of the greater question of race. There was one other factor—his mild manner and his conscience prevent him from helping in questionable situations in which a more ruthless person would have gone the limit.

When I called at Mr. Kendall's office he was busily engaged in preparing letters to be typed and sent to the people in his division. He was filled with grief over his defeat. He had deserved reelection on the record of his services. "Twenty years in politics—fourteen years on the ward committee; I had never refused a possible request." It was a bewildering situation. He could not accept defeat yet. He was sending out letters to tell the Jews what he had done for them—had he not employed Jewish secretaries in his office? (One of them wrote an ardent letter to her people in the division in Mr. Kendall's behalf.) I tried to say that the election was over—an appeal is useless now. But he could not listen—"No, I am the president of a boys' club and active in various community projects. I want to know just what the people think of me. I'll quit everything if they don't appreciate my services." I paid him a last farewell and departed thinking that politics is a strenuous game, disquieting and thankless. It is difficult for a gentleman to survive—unless he is a hell of a fighter. And I remembered how, years ago, Edmund Burke was turned down by the sheriffs of Bristol.

NICHOLAS FISHBOURNE

Man of Action

>>>->>>->>>->>>->>>->>>->>>->>>->>>->>>->>><<<-<<<-<<<-<<<-<<<-<<<-<<<-<<<-<<<-<<<-<<<-<<<

NICHOLAS FISHBOURNE knows nothing of books on political science—he was forced to quit school at the age of eleven to help his mother; but that was nearly thirty years ago. Since then he has acquired much first-hand knowledge about politics and law in face-to-face situations. Like another politician, Edmund Burke, he is a profound believer in prescription, "never entirely nor at once to depart from antiquity." Yet his salty worldly wisdom is terse and pungent, and he is apt to depart abruptly from custom if the peculiar exigencies of a hard-pressed election battle or a sudden raid on his policy writers indicates that a new line of attack or defense is needed.

One night, seated comfortably in his political club back in the mill section, I produced an old torn volume of "Solid for Mulhooly." Nick is a friend of mine and listens courteously to any suggestions that I make. I opened the book to Chapter VIII and read the sayings that one of Mulhooly's disciples had jotted down fifty years ago. "Which of these are good in Philadelphia today?" I asked. He sat back in his big chair, his men deployed about him on both sides, and meditatively puffed his cigar as I read. Here are the maxims that he had tested in his laboratory, his district, and had already incorporated in his own (unwritten) political catechism as containing sound political truth:

"The government means, not those who vote, but those who receive, count, and return the votes."

"One election officer well in hand is worth a score of voters on the half shell."

"Elections are ratification meetings which we hold to endorse our nominations."

"The result of an election is only a question of figures. A stroke of the pen before the figure 99 is as good as the votes of a hundred millionaire taxpayers, if you're smart enough to get away with it."

"What we want all the time is a solid election-officer, a solid jury, a solid judge, and a solid governor, in case of slips, and the people may be d****d!"

"That man who intimates that I can be bought insults me—not the fellow who talks biz."

"Give the people plenty of taffy and the newspapers plenty of advertising—then help yourself to anything that's lying around loose."

"A chunk of meat will cure the bark and the bite of a dog; therefore if you don't know how to silence a Reformer, it's your own fault."

After I had read these maxims, Nick commented on the importance of election officers. "You know yourself the value of owning the election board. Where would I have been last time if the judge hadn't been my man?"

This last election was only a month ago, and I had spent four hours in the polling place observing Nick, the master mechanic, operate a voting machine. I had arrived at nine—two hours after the polls had opened. The polling place is on other days the front room of the house of a loyal family with seven votes. They are patriotic and willing to rent out their best room to Nick (for twenty-five dollars) on primary and election days. It was ample in size for the huge mechanical vote tabulator, and a long table at which were seated the two ward committeemen; the lean, ramrod-like "custodian of records" with pale sunken cheeks and heavy dark eyebrows; three party workers; the ward leader's father, who was living over the battles of his youth when Penrose was in the legislature and Iz Durham gave the orders; and the two Pinchot watchers—the opposition. (Of course the judge of election and the inspectors were there, too.)

Nick had noticed me standing on the curb. He called me in. As I stood in the doorway, he looked at the Pinchot watchers and peremptorily said, "You fellows don't care if the Professor comes in here, do you?" (Of course, the law says—but why mention the law? It is not so much the law that counts as custom and personality.) They assented, so I took a place at the opposite end of the table from the small, wiry, dark-visaged judge. I lent the senior of the Pinchot watchers my morning newspaper, and won the good will of the strangers.

While I observed, 177 men and women voted. Of that number, 11 people voted without assistance; the 166 were assisted—partly because the machines were new to these people, but more truly because Nick was their friend, and they wanted to show him that their vote was his. Voting was almost continuous while I was there. A voter would come in and Nick would call him by name—not once did he fail in this. While the clerk was writing down the name, the voter would ask help —say that he or she could not work the machine. The judge of elections would look at Nick and say, "Who do you want to assist you?" Sometimes the person would point to Nick, and other times he would call him by name. With a practiced hand Nick would pull aside the curtain and the two would enter. In a jiffy the lever would be pulled and they would come out. I timed Fishbourne on voting the voters. Once it took him twenty seconds, another time it was twenty-four, and a third time it was thirty. It was never more than a minute and a half save twice when there were mild arguments behind the curtain. The matter was adjusted by Nick's turning down the meaningful pointers and the "voter" pulling the lever that registered a vote for the names below the turned pointers. This was voting with dispatch, since it was a primary election and straight-ticket voting was not possible, and nineteen individual pointers had to be turned down. When Nick noticed my watch, he said, "My time is pretty good, ain't it—the machine works fine today."

As he came out of the curtains and approached the ballot box he would hand the paper ballot to the voter (there was a paper ballot too—the machine was not big enough to provide space for all the candidates), and say, "Here, put this in the ballot box—it's your ballot." The voter would grab the ballot and shove it through the opening. The election official or Nick would ask the voter to tear the coupon off the ballot before he

150

went into the booth. The corner coupon was to prevent chain voting; the number entered on the voting lists when the citizen received his ballot should have been compared with the ballot that he was about to deposit in the ballot box, and if the two numbers were identical the stub was to be removed before the ballot was deposited in the urn. It is painfully obvious that the separation of the coupon from the ballot before voting completely nullifies the value of the coupon and defeats the purpose of the legislature in providing for it. None of the boys knew what the coupon was for, nor did they wonder about it. They did know, however, that if a ballot were found in the box with its number attached, the judge of elections would be subject to a fine of $10.00. To forestall that possibility, the numbered coupon was detached early in the voting process.

Sometimes when an alleged voter asked for assistance, the opposition watcher would protest and remind the judge that a voter is legally entitled to aid in voting only (1) if he cannot read the names on the ballot or voting machine, or (2) if because of physical disability he cannot mark the ballot unaided. Often before the opposition watcher had completed his explanation, Nick would tell the watcher to "shut up." Or the watcher might say that the voter might be instructed, not assisted. Then Nick might take the small demonstration machine and appear to demonstrate its operation to the voter. These mechanical inventions are more complicated than they look. The franchise-holder still asked for help; the men or women would swear to their disability on the Bible, and select Nick—or occasionally it was Joe, Nick's partner—to assist them.

Nick's attitude toward the Pinchot watchers interested me. Instead of being conciliatory, he was domineering and insolent. Yet when he ordered sandwiches and pop at noon, he supplied them, too. His polling-place technique was good, and, regardless of laws, he dominated the picture.

One of those assisted was an aged Catholic priest who brought along his own machine operator; and three others who were helped were party workers. Nick just was not taking any chances. That night he was able to report to his leader 319 votes for the organization, and 17 votes for the opposition candidates. (No more zero divisions for Nick—they are the kind that get you into trouble and cause investigations. And no more ballot-box stuffing either—"This is 1932—things are different now.")

Nick usually employs from ten to twenty men, and one or two women at a primary or an election. The number depends on the nature of the fight and the number of unemployed in the district. The majority of workers are paid $5.00 or $10.00 a day. A few more influential ones that can carry a handful of votes with them are paid $20, and one incipient rebellion was entirely dissipated before it materialized by paying $100 to its leader. These workers call on the voters at their homes and say, "Nick wants you to come and vote." Every registered voter is visited and the appeal is always effective except in the case of one old man from Ireland; he moves about with difficulty, and will not

152

budge an inch toward the polls unless Nick, in person and with his automobile, calls for him. The major part of the money spent for workers is given as a largesse by a sovereign to his deserving people on the eve of a victory—$100 is given to Nick by the leader at a primary election and $75 at a general election. The exact amount varies, but this is the average over a period of twelve years. The difference is made up out of Nick's pocket.

This pocket has been amply supplied with cash ever since Nick made his first entry into politics. Before that time he had had money, too, but in more uncertain amounts. He was originally proprietor of a combination pool room and blind pig. However, then as now, his main source of revenue was gambling. As a youngster of twenty-three he had friends—many of them, he said, "but they didn't mean a damn thing in a pinch!" He was arrested and he promptly turned to his division leader. This man removed himself from politics by telling Nick to go to hell—that he would not help a law violator. This was like lashing Nick across the face with a whip. He wriggled out of his difficulty and thereafter devoted himself to politics. He had a new ambition now. He would become a division leader himself and protect his own interests. By promises and cash he won over one of the key men of the leader he was going to defeat, and he systematically told the electorate what he stood for; above all he emphasized two words—*personal service*. (An examination of his life from that time on reveals that no Roosevelt or Wilson ever lived up to his platform as did Nick to his.) In a poll of about seven hundred votes, he won by more than one hundred.

153

(Since that time the only candidate for public office that has caused him any serious concern was Al Smith.) He now carries his district in his pocket.

This is why the leader of the ward welcomes him to the fold, as one of the band of brothers, though he fears him and profoundly dislikes him. For Nick is not the abject order-man that all good politicians must be. Besides, Nick has possibilities that no one can foresee. His name is already a tower of strength in the ward, and, if this persistent conniver is not stopped by a bullet or permanently lodged behind the gray walls of some Old Bailey, he may become ward leader. However, there are times when the Boss, though often suspicious of Nick's increasing power, is profoundly for him. A block of nearly six hundred votes delivered each time like clockwork will help any ward leader to forgive much.

Nick feels the leader's attitude and knows of the jealousy he foments on crucial occasions among the other division leaders. It quite bewilders him and fills him with sorrow. "I don't want to harm anybody. I just want to do good for people. I will never take Mac's job. If he will make me a magistrate I can make him the most powerful ward leader in the city. Every time a person is brought before me, if the charges against him ain't too bad, I would say, 'See here, I'm letting you off easy. Not because I don't think you are guilty, not because you are well-dressed, or good-looking, but just because of the Republican party. Thank Mac ———, your ward leader, for your freedom. Don't thank me.' "

154

NICHOLAS FISHBOURNE

I do not know just when Nick gave up the pool room and became the one-man convoy for a truck laden with liquor. He trailed the truck in a fast roadster and carried a shotgun across his lap, and a roll of bills in his pocket. "I was prepared for hijackers and government officers." But the risks were too great, even for a man of action. He became a bootlegger next, selling to smaller dealers. One of these was Joe, his partner on the ward committee. Nick told Joe that he did not want to make a nickel on him. He charged $32 a case; Joe thinks the stuff cost $19, and so he gave up the business. Liquor is bulky, so Nick transferred his major attention to gambling. He entered the number racket before it became the $1,000,000 big-time racket that Charles F. Lee, former captain of the vice squad, stated that it is in Philadelphia today.

One registration night I observed Nick and his men at work. I told him that some of my friends had asked me to explain the number game to them and I was not able to do it. Without saying a word to me he turned and called, "Tiff!" A small, dark, secretive individual came to the hallway where we were standing. "Let me see your book," he said, and Tiff drew forth a small book with paper covers and pages the width of a cigarette paper and about five inches long. Nick succinctly explained the lottery and said that he was in it as banker, in order to give employment to some of his men during the depression. His political influence with police, magistrates, and judges is most vital here, for when one of his men is arrested, Nick can invariably fix it.

Nearly a year later I was talking to Nick at the club, in the inner room where all the party heroes of the past were looking down upon us from their high frames on the wall. It was late and, after we had talked an hour, he asked me if I wanted a ride. We got into his car and drove a few blocks to the home of one of his lieutenants, who joined us; then we started for another section of the city—five wards away. We stopped a half-block from a small corner cigar store. On the way there Nick's man Friday had been dispatched to a near-by point, where a buxom woman lived who sells numbers for Nick.

When we arrived and I saw the man that greeted Nick I thought of what Nick had said several times on the way over that night about this agent, Blum—"He is a great, powerful man. He is even bigger than I am." This man was monstrously large—he had massive, hulking shoulders that sloped, a bull neck, and a great bald head shaped like a torpedo. His eyes peered out from bushy eyebrows; his skin was yellow; if he had not been so big he might have been Lon Chaney in disguise. He was standing on the curb when we arrived. He had been waiting for Nick, for that day he had been arrested. The man paid little attention to me; I had been introduced as Professor Salter—"a personal friend of mine." He spoke falteringly and in a low voice almost in a whisper.

We three walked into the rear room of the store—past a middle room where four men were playing cards. We sat down at a round table with a soiled white table-cloth on it. There was a high-school student there trying to study Caesar, although he was more interested

156

in following the conversation. The big man asked him to get out. The boy did not move. The man started to rise; the boy dodged and ran through the door, which he closed behind him. Then Blum again started to explain the situation, when he stopped, looked at me, and said, "Who is this man, Nick?" Nick said, "The Professor." Blum sneered, "Professor Cook, eh?" Nick abruptly reassured him and the man continued, "I was arrested [for selling numbers]. Paid the social officer $60. The officer had the charge dropped by the magistrate. Officer told me that they would put it down as playing the horses or anything. I guess I must have mentioned it while there was some loafer in the store. Some one told the officer that he had given me a special break. He came back, wanted to return my money, and arrest me all over again. I talked him out of it. I thought you ought to fix this special officer so he won't bother me again. He knows who you are, I think."

Nick broke in, "No, he don't know me."

But Blum answered, "Yes, he told me your initials, and he said that you were a big-hearted fellow." Nick was satisfied with the description. "Well, maybe he does know me." Nick promised to secure protection for him, and credited him with $30—half the bribe. The man then paid Nick $18, the balance on the day's takings, and we left.

As we rode away, Nick ruminated on the perfidy of human nature among those ubiquitous individuals that wear police uniforms. Two weeks ago a special officer had gambled with Nick on numbers and won $475; a week later he lost $620, and refused to pay. There were other cases; "an honest man is helpless when dealing with the police. I buy them, and they won't stay bought!"

The next day I was in another world. I was one of a select group that was addressed by Kern Dodge, director of public safety. After he had finished denouncing the Communists for holding meetings on the square, I asked, "To what extent, if at all, are the police working with the number-writers?" He promptly answered, "Of course some are working in the number racket; they are both collectors and pay-off men. My job is to find out who they are." But the problem is difficult, for gambling, like the love of liquor and the desire for sex experience, is commonly found in the generality of mankind; and the only equipment required is a name in which the gamblers have confidence, and a book not many times larger than a book of stamps. Thus it is that Nick, in backing the number racket, is catering to a public though illegal demand.

Nick has a strain of temper in his otherwise placid being that flares up uncontrollably at times. He can usually engineer his operations in the Roaring Twenty-first District without calling on his ward leader, but one time he asked him for a favor which the leader refused to grant. "This made me so mad that I told him to take his job in City Hall and go to hell. All that I wanted him to do was to speak to a judge that I couldn't speak to in behalf of a young man that had stolen a mere $200. He might have needed the money and didn't mean any harm by it at all. Besides, restitution was made. In the Al Smith election, McTee [the leader] didn't know until after the voting who I was voting for. However, when I brought my returns in that night at the club there were more than seventy committeemen with the Boss. I started to go out and he said, 'Wait a minute.' He read off the returns and he said, 'Some of you men making $4,000 and $5,000 a year ought to be ashamed of yourselves.' I said, 'Mac, you don't need to say that,' and I went home." (The Al Smith fight was easily the most difficult one that he had ever waged around the polls. His people are mostly Irish and of Irish extraction and there were at least two reasons why they were for Al. However, his people knew that Nick was wet, and that he was for the entire Republican ticket. When they demurred, he reminded them of past favors, and asked what Al Smith had ever done for them. He capped his talk with, "If you vote for Al, go to him at Albany the next time you want something done." Nick's man Hoover got over four hundred votes; Al received thirty-three.)

The last time that one of his men was arrested for selling lottery number tickets, Nick went to the police station to get the copy of the charge. Captain Nit refused to accomodate Nick. He said that he was tired of having his men arrest gamblers and then having a politician get them off. Nick told the captain to go to hell, and asked to use the telephone. He said that he had a legal right to the copy—which he had—and that it was for the magistrate to decide whether he would sign it or not. Before Nick had completed his call to the superintendent of the police, Captain Nit gave him the copy.

Early in his political career Nick was an employee in an office in City Hall. The official head of this office is a powerful ward leader, but the actual managing director of the work and employees is a trained accountant. Nick usually had station-house calls that required his presence at the police station before he went to the City Hall. One morning he arrived at the Hall at eleven o'clock. The director said that he would have to be there on time in the future. Nick replied that he had been busy serving the party in the division. "You don't suppose I carry my people at the polls because they are interested in my ticket, do you?" Two days later he was two hours late again. The director started censoring Nick, who held up his hand, "See here, I worked a hell of a lot harder before Magistrate X than you have been working here at the Hall. I'll tell the leader about your crabbing—you don't know what it is all about!" Nick started to go into the inner office where the big fellow often met his friends. He was stopped by the director and assured that hereafter it would be all right for him to serve his friends before reporting for work.

When Nick told me this story about getting his personal freedom in politics, I said, "I suppose from then on you never appeared before twelve." He said, "What?" I repeated my statement. He replied, "I never appeared again—except to get my pay check. You must talk up, or, by God, you don't get no place! I found that out long ago." I commented, "However, it might be better to meet your opposition with a rapier instead of a meat axe." He smiled, "Professor, I got only one weapon, but it's good for the work I got to do."

160

Nick Fishbourne takes the same sort of pride in his art as any artist might in his. The source of Nick's power is the ballot box, and he does not neglect it. Heart and brain, bone and sinew are thrown into the contests there. One other maxim of which he partially approved is not quite correct. "It is therefore more important for you to see the election officers than the voters of your district." He added this to it: "I do both, and that is why they can never beat me—you know some of the things I do for my people."

In the first place, though Nick is not jovial by nature, the least he does is to speak whenever he meets a person that lives in his district. I know, too, that the little boys for streets around look up to him as a Robin Hood or the hero of their dreams. Once, for a while, he wore a soft gray Stetson that was turned up, instead of down, in the front. Soon all the young male voters of 1942–1943 were wearing soft gray hats turned up in front. Nick's benefactions in his home country are real and substantial, the sort one can see and feel. First, there are the merchants in his district—they are assessed an annual mercantile tax of from $20 to $60, depending upon their reported sales. The ones that took their assessments to Nick instead of to City Hall got them reduced through some legerdemain all Nick's own, to from $2.00 to $8.00. Once I found him very much perturbed. The son of a merchant had tried to pay his father's tax at City Hall. He was asked to pay the correct amount instead of the sum that he had paid the first year. When he came to Nick about it, Nick wanted to know why he had not come to him originally, and the son said that he had thought he could take care of the matter himself, but now he begged for Nick's help. He got it and was warned not to fool around with these things himself.

Just three weeks ago Sunday when the club was closed there were seventeen or eighteen men from the district in Nick's house. He gave each of them a shot of liquor and then took them over to the Rumanian restaurant at Thirty-third and M Streets, and bought each of them a dinner at a dollar a plate. He often lets a fellow have a dollar or two without expecting to see the person return it in cash. He likes to help people out, and besides, "doing good" is the greater part of his political capital. At that time and for at least six weeks back, he had been giving four families $3.00 a week. When the poor need a friend he does not fail them. Last Christmas he gave out eighty-one baskets of groceries to destitute families in his neighborhood; each basket contained two loaves of bread, five pounds of potatoes, six cans of vegetable soup, one can of beans, one pound of coffee, two pounds of sugar, one can of milk, one large can of tomatoes, one can of tomato paste, one box of salt, one pound of lard, and one three-pound ham. Although he has twenty workers he took these baskets around himself (on Christmas Eve) and wished each family a Merry Christmas. Around Easter time there was much suffering in his section; people needed food, coal, and money for rent. Nick saw that something had to be done. He obtained a special permit to hold a boxing bout in his ward. The tickets were sold at $1.00 apiece. He personally sold 250 to eight men who wanted to stand well with him; his workers sold the rest. As a result of this venture he was able to distribute $600 in cash and supplies the following weeks.

However, his greatest role is that of buffer between the voter and the law. He is so successful in this that some of his envious colleagues on the ward committee call him "Old Eagle Eye." People in other districts know so much of his skill as an adjuster—"a fixer," to be more exact—that they will send for him when trapped by the police instead of for their more uncertain district leader at home. When Nick helps them, he always explains that he is doing it for their own leader and not for them. Just the same, these far-reaching services arouse the jealousy of the other members of the ward committee and the fear of the ward leader. (The leader is always worried when any other person becomes too powerful.) Hence the monicker, "Old Eagle Eye," for Nick, and it is always said with a tinge of sarcasm. He is puzzled at this attitude. "All I want to do is help someone," he says.

One of his unique cases before a magistrate was one in which Dan Jones, a negro, was arrested for selling lottery tickets on the Maryland horse races. Dan had a friend that knows Nick, and arranged for Nick to get him out. Nick obtained the signature of a magistrate to a "copy of the charge." This permitted the negro to leave the police station in Nick's custody until the date set for the hearing. The negro promised to be there, but the case against him looked bad; he did not know Nick's special abilities with police and magistrates, so he skipped the city. The grapevine brought this word to Nick, on the morning of the day set for the hearing.

This might have been an embarrassing predicament for one less resourceful. But Nick got one of his colored stand-bys to substitute for Dan Jones when Dan's name was called in court. He stood before "His Honor," and, after hearing Nick explain the case, was "discharged," as Nick had said he would be. This happened a year ago, but even today to recount this tale gives Nick the nearest approach to a belly laugh of which one so naturally sober is capable. "The magistrate doesn't know the difference yet!" and then he adds, "The cop did, but I gave him $10.00 to keep his mouth shut."

But the case that best revealed Nick's ability to produce results in a magistrate's court arose in connection with two overloaded trucks. A friend of his owned them and he came to Nick shortly after the arrests were made. The case was to come up on a Tuesday morning before Nick's boon companion, the enthusiastic poker player, Magistrate McGannon. This judge is one that will go far for a friend, and Nick had already explained the difficulty to him. As I accompanied him to the magistrate's court I was told what the verdict would be. "The judge will give M. $40.20 [fine] on each truck—$80.40 in all, because there will be an assistant city solicitor there to check up on this, and then after the hearing he will cut the fine to $11.50; he will pay only the cost." (And this is exactly what happened.)

When we arrived, the small, office-like court was jammed with about forty people, and court was in session. Nick took a place on the platform beside the judge. I stood some ten feet away in front of the judge, but there were so many people in between us that only by standing on tiptoes could I see the dispenser of justice and favors. Nick noticed my difficulty and he called out for me to come up on the platform. "You can see better." In a short time I was standing directly behind the magistrate's chair—an excellent place for observation. The owner of the trucks had not realized that his loads exceeded the legal maximum, etc. He had been arrested for this offence before? Yes. He was warned and fined, as Nick had said he would be. The hearings were adjourned and Nick, the owner of the truck, and the assistant city solicitor stood outside. The solicitor pointed to our friend the politician and said, "He is the one you want to thank—he got you off easy. [Nick had spoken a word concerning the man's character in court.] Thank him." The solicitor did not fully realize the extent of Nick's influence in that case, but the owner of the truck did. Nick went into the back room behind the court and there he and the magistrate straightened this case out to the satisfaction of everyone except the city solicitor's man, and he need never know.

McGannon and Nick are such good friends that often on week-ends they will play stud poker right around the clock—from four on Saturday to four on Sunday. Nick hates Coe, however, the magistrate from his ward— because "he wouldn't cooperate properly on a liquor case and I told him to go to hell." Since then they have been sworn enemies. If Nick has a case before Coe he has his partner on the party committee handle it. One time at a hearing before McGannon a girl whose status was being decided handed him a note. McGannon read it and said, "Here is a note for you, Nick." The note read,

DEAR JUDGE:
   This girl is a friend of mine. Take care of her.

COE.

   "Of course," said Nick, in telling the story, "the judge knows that I don't think much of Coe." Then he added, "McGannon just held the girl under $1,000 for court, but I got him to reverse his decision. Said that the girl lived in the ward, and that she deserved help. McGannon said, 'All right, Nick, I'll do it for you.' She was held for further hearing on $300 bail. I signed it. The girl was discharged at a further hearing. I wouldn't strike at Coe through a girl."

   One day when I observed Nick in court, the case concerned a boy fourteen years old who had been caught stealing from a warehouse. He was discharged at the hearing. Nick told the Judge. "I don't care whether he is guilty or not—he is only a boy, after all." McGannon let the boy off with a warning.

   Another case that Nick took in hand brought out the difference in the attitude of two judges of the X court—both of whom are actual though not the titular leaders of wards. A young negro was held for court by a magistrate on a charge of fornication, rape, and bastardy. His parents came to Nick; they wanted him to get the boy out of prison. Nick went to judge number 1, who was a close friend of his, and this judge made a telephone call that got the boy released until his trial at eleven o'clock on Friday of that week. However, at eleven Nick was unfortunately busy at the coroner's office concerning a man held for manslaughter. He had sent word to the

166

presiding judge in the negro rape case to wait for him, but the judge (number 2) left at twelve noon and issued a bench warrant for the colored boy. When Nick arrived, the boy had already been committed to prison. Nick promptly got in touch with judge number 1. This judge called the clerk of court at 10 p.m. on Friday. Nick went to the clerk's house and got the release order. He then went to the county prison and got the boy released until further hearing. When judge number 2, the one that had issued the warrant, learned of it, "he got sore and bawled hell out of both the other judge and the clerk. He insisted that the negro remain in jail or put up $600 bail—real bail, too." Judge number 1 was appealed to again—he wanted the man released but the clerk would not release him; later he did. "And I did not enter any bail. The boy was supposed to be in jail all the time. I promised to have him in court the day of the hearing." That day clerk Langer took the boy, sneaked him back to the cell room at the court. The judge number 2 says, "Hanley [the colored boy]—where is he?" Clerk answers, "Your Honor, he is here in custody." The judge asked to have him brought in. The boy denied the paternity at the hearing, but the girl was there with the child. The judge put a $2.00 a week support order against Hanley. Nick explained that he had gone to all this trouble because "even a nigger don't like to stay in jail a minute longer than he has to." This sort of imagination is what makes him fight so energetically for his personal freedom. Then, too, there is the sheer joy; he feels the keen delight in outsmarting judge number 2 that he would feel in winning an important billiard match with his best friends there to see him do it. Only this sort of battle is even more significant than billiards or poker, for, to Nick, politics is the greatest game of all; and just what he means by politics his daily actions reveal.

One morning I chanced to meet Nick on the sixth floor of City Hall. He was talking to two detectives and the representatives of a downtown men's store. He called me over to the conference—one of the myriad that daily take place in the broad corridors just outside courtrooms, the district attorney's office, and other key places. Two of Nick's constituents—boys about twenty—had been arrested for stealing two overcoats. They had walked out with the new coats on their backs, leaving their old ones in exchange. They were detected because they had inadvertently left a price tag on one of the coats. Nick was trying to get the men from the store not to appear in court against the boys. He argued that the boys were young, that they would never go into the store again, and besides, "Business is bad now, I will pay for the coats, and you will have made a sale." Not at first, but finally, the store men agreed.

This was the sort of case in which Nick called in one of his attorneys. (He has attorney number 1 for the more legitimate cases, and number 2 for the more difficult ones. This was a number 1 case.) While Nick was maneuvering about, his lawyer said to me, "The boys owe me a fee of $45, and they must pay that before their case comes up or I will tell the judge to sock them." (Nick gets 50 per cent of the fee from the cases that he turns over to his attorneys, and he also receives a split

168

on the fee for a bond.) The families of the two boys were there in a huddle, with worried looks on their faces. It had been twenty-one years since they had left the Russian homeland, and, as they crowded against the opposite wall of the corridor, they never took their eyes off Nick—he was their benefactor, the Mayor of the City, and the Constitution of the United States all in one. They would raise the money for the coats and, although the words were not spoken, they were none the less felt; they would vote for Nick always and tell their friends.

One morning Nick was called to the Forty-third and Tuppen Street police station; a man was held for having killed an iceman with his truck. There were two ambulance-chasing attorneys after the case and three relatives of the prisoner. One of the relatives pointed out Nick and said, "Take him." The other relatives asked Mr. Fishbourne if he were an attorney; he said that he was not but that he thought he could handle the case. The attorneys were heartsick at the possible loss of a fee. They vigorously protested. Nick did not argue with them; he ignored them. He told the relatives that he was going home, that he would be there for thirty minutes, and that, if they wanted him, to call within that time. He had no sooner reached home than a call came. He promptly returned and found that the prisoner was being held for court without bail. He thereupon got an allowance—that is, the privilege of taking the prisoner, in custody of a policeman, to the district attorney's office, where he arranged for bail. The bail was fixed at $1500 and finally approved by a court.

A few days later the matter came up before the coroner. Nick was there with his attorney number 2. The attorney, a Mr. Visor, questioned the prisoner, but the truck-driver got "all balled up on the witness stand, although we had coached him on his story, and he had known it by heart before he got on the stand. For instance, the truck that killed the man crushed him against a telephone pole on the left of the truck. The truck was going south, and when Mr. Visor would ask the man which way he turned, he would always say that he turned left. Visor wanted him to answer the question again. The plaintiff's lawyer objected, but the coroner (who had been spoken to by the ward leader) "allowed the question." The case was continued for a further hearing, and then it was discharged by the coroner. "All that was required was a few dollars for a few officers and clerks. Of course, you know how that is." I thought that I knew, but one night at a propitious moment I asked Mr. Visor for a bill of particulars. Here it is:

Detective Craig..................................	$ 10.00
Tinke and Company (2 motor-cycle policemen).....	$ 20.00
Tim C., a deputy corner—investigator told the coroner the death was accidental, etc............	$ 15.00
Ditto later....................................	$ 5.00
Ditto later, another...........................	$ 5.00
Irish Sergeant at Forty-third and Tuppen Streets. (He was nice to us—gave us the records. Told us who we could fix, etc.)..........................	$ 5.00
In addition I paid $135 toward the funeral expenses of the dead man.................................	$135.00

NICHOLAS FISHBOURNE

The most amazing thing about Nick is his energy. This enables him to live two full lives, while lesser politicians live but one. To know him is to be reminded of Prince Henry's description of Hotspur: "I am not yet of Percy's mind, the Hotspur of the north; he that kills me some six or seven dozen of Scots at a breakfast, washes his hands, and says to his wife 'Fie upon this quiet life! I want work.' "

Nick has a massive frame and were it not for his blond hair he could double for Jack Dempsey. I have often seen him in late afternoons at Irish George Henley's gymnasium, throwing a medicine ball. He plays with two men, neither of whom is underweight, and then, when they are exhausted, he throws the huge balls to fresh ones. He has a shower, a rubdown, and he is ready for what the night may bring.

His vigor would be less incomprehensible if his sleeping hours were as regular as the voting in his district. His hours are necessarily uncertain, but, fortunately, he sleeps like an innocent babe whenever his head touches a pillow. He chooses his food with intelligence, and drinks sparingly; if it were not for the social amenities, he would not drink at all.

Mr. Fishbourne has never married. He lives in a small, modest house on a narrow street; his front room is large and the partition that originally separated this room from the next one has been removed. It is comfortably furnished with an unusual number of overstuffed chairs. The one decoration is a high photograph in a gilt frame. It is a picture of an impressive-looking man in a uniform of some sort, Nick's father, who died many years ago. Now Nick and his pleasant and shrewd mother live alone—save that they are never alone.

He spends much of his time at the club in his own ward. (He is a member of four other political clubs, for important contacts are political power.) But when the ward leader is at the club, Nick is not there; whatever his world is, he must be the sun in that world; he cannot remain in the reflected glory of another man. By nature and training he dominates situations and men. His personal power is that of a slumbering grizzly. It is felt by those that come in contact with him. It is concentrated strength and energy. His power is never diffused over a wide surface; it is focused on the precise crux of the problem confronting him. His "is the arduous greatness of things done." Of course, he likes to talk, and he invariably has something to say; but conversation is not his forte; his success reveals that "gold were as good as twenty orators." I have never seen him excited. In the presence of his leader he is subdued, but fortunately his leader is an old man and rarely makes more than a perfunctory call at the club in the evening, and always comes at the same hour. Nick knows his habits as I know those of my dog. He arrives just after the boss departs. He never speaks ill of his titular leader, however; his respect for position and ceremonial is too deeply ingrained. (One day Nick went to New York to see a political friend, and together they made a business call on a judge. Nick's friend was personally acquainted with the judge, slapped him on the back in raucous good fellowship, and to Nick's astonishment called him by a profane name in extending his greeting. The judge

172

responded in kind, granted the favor asked, and the two departed. Nick described this meeting with great interest; he said that this way of treating a judge was something new to him, and that it couldn't be done in Philadelphia.)

One night I called at his home about nine o'clock. He had asked me to come, but he was asleep in a rear room when I arrived. His mother informed me that he was to be called at eleven. As I waited a boy of twelve or so came to the door and asked if Mr. Fishbourne would come over to his home—his father wanted to see him. Mrs. Fishbourne said that Nick was sleeping and she would tell him when he got up. (After the boy had gone, she told me that one of Nick's men had struck a small child, the boy's brother, with Nick's car that afternoon. Nick had taken the child to the hospital.) An hour later in the evening, the boy returned. He said that his father had to go to bed soon so that he could get up early in the morning to go to work. (His father was a dock laborer.) He wanted Nick to come over to his house. Mrs. Fishbourne asked the boy to have his father come over, but the boy answered that he did not want to.

Shortly after Nick woke up, the boy came again, and Nick told him that he wanted the father to come right over. In a few minutes the father did come. He was a young German who had four children. He spoke English with difficulty, and seemed embarrassed at being here in this strange house. He said, "I know you and you know me. I leave it to you to take care of my boy. Someone else—I get a lawyer. Not you. I leave it to you. I live eleven years on this street. First, I don't want anything bad wrong with my boy. I don't want any trouble with you."

This was on the whole as fine a tribute as one neighbor could pay another, yet, to my surprise, Nick failed to respond adequately at once to this generous offer, which revealed so clearly the man's implicit trust in Nick. Instead of saying "All right" and that he would see to everything, as he had previously assured me he would, he hesitated, became almost evasive, and said that no lawyer would be needed, but that if one were he would get one. A few minutes later he told the distraught father that he would see that the boy was well taken care of. This was what the father wanted to hear. He bravely crossed the room—he was very timid—and shook hands with the politician before he went out.

Nick again told me that he had already provided for competent medical care for the boy at the hospital, that he was not badly hurt; and then we talked of politics. But I continued to think of the father, a foreigner, so concerned with maintaining the friendship and good will of a man who had befriended him in the past, that he humbly asked for what another would have demanded. The circumstances and attitude of mind reminded one of a feudal system—a system of society where inherent rights did not exist but only favors granted by a beneficient lord.

In walking about Nick's bailiwick I have approached his home from every angle, and twenty times I have asked people in houses, or on the street, where Nick Fishbourne lived; and every time I was told. He is a person that bulks large in his community. In this sketch

I have mentioned only a fraction of Nick's countless favors that make life more tolerable for the people among whom he lives. (Others of a more spectacular nature, and the positions he has held in City Hall during these last sixteen years, I shall not recount, lest I identify him. It is sufficient to observe that he is securely attached to the public pay roll; his $2,200 a year job, plus his imagination and confidence, is usually worth $4,000 to $5,000 to him.) The activities that I have listed are basic to Nick's life; they reveal both the problems arising among his people and the manner in which he obtains money to help his constituents and to help himself. Both the favors and the money are essential for continued success in the party organization. Words are not enough in this sphere of politics; deeds are required. A politician without money is as helpless as a soldier on a battlefield without bullets. If Nick has a flair for lawbreaking, then so do the effective majority in his district. At least they are interested in having their bellies full, and a roof over their heads, and they care little about the source of the money. The reformers and independents that talk of law and the constitution and the city charter are not effectively appealing to these people. To them a free exercise of the franchise is not so vital a thing as bread and butter, bacon and beans. At best the good to be derived from a free vote is not easily associated with the here and now. Hunger or a possible prison sentence are not distant and remote. A person without social vision or imagination can readily choose, when in some difficulty, between being a free and sovereign person or having a free and sovereign vote. In helping him to choose the former, Nick is not fitting him for someday choosing the latter, but he is making his present life more endurable—a life which, both by nature and training, he is destined to live. It is for this reason that, to an overwhelming majority in his district, he is the neighborhood patriot. (However, now as the bitterness of the depression continues, and as President Roosevelt does the social work for many that Nick does for a favored few, and as Democracy's leader dramatically tells the people what he is doing for them, the problems confronting every Republican leader are magnified. Nick is no exception to this statement. His people are restless, and are turning toward new political gods; it inevitably follows that Nick is restive too; he wonders when Roosevelt and the Democratic appeal will weaken, and how long he himself can hold out. He has never lost yet, but to an ardent minority he is becoming less the patriot and more the tyrant.)

The last time that Nick and I talked was one of the very few times that he asked my advice. His question indicates the increased irritation felt in his life these days. He had taken me aside from his small group and asked, "Do you think it would be a good idea for me to sock X on the jaw?" [X, a political leader who had been denying favors.] I replied, "Force never settles anything." He smilingly said, "I don't know. When I was a lot younger, I had a good friend by the name of Tom. We were in the numbers game together. My mother knew nothing about it and used to wonder what I did while I was away from home. One day she asked Tom. He told her that I was a gambler. When I came home

176

she cried. At first she wouldn't tell me what was wrong, and then she did. I walked out without saying a word. Tom was standing on a street corner. I warned him, then I socked him. He fell to the curb. When he came to, he came over and said, 'I had it coming to me.' And do you know we were good friends from then on. He was dependable after that.''

Nick's weaknesses as a leader are his lack of tact, social insight, integrity, patience, and an ability to cooperate with equals and superiors. In short, he is too much the "big I Am." In listing his assets and strength it should be first of all noted that he is a promoter of money; that he has superb energy, resourcefulness, great courage; he has also persistence, a good memory, a capacity for details in organization, and goodness of heart. However, though he will always sigh for new worlds to conquer, his own limitations, and the pressure of public opinion— it beats down more brightly on the higher places—will probably confine him to this one sphere of which he is now so energetic a part.

* * * * * * *

The greater part of this sketch appeared in *Harper's Magazine* for March, 1933. At my suggestion the editor sent a copy of this issue to Nick. Some weeks later Nick wrote me the following letter. The italics at the end are his. The letter stands as Nick wrote it save for names which have been omitted.

March, 30, 1933

My dear Professor:

I sincerely hope that this letter finds you enjoying the best of health.

I believe that —— —— and myself also enjoyed reading your article on Nicholas Fishbourne as much as your friends and other interested readers did. It certainly was interesting to me, indeed.

Some of these little incidents seemed a bit familiar to me, but, perhaps, I have an unknown twin brother somewhere. A few of these little stories about Nick certainly gave me a big hearty laugh and I can assure you that if you had heard my "ha-ha," you would have thought it was old "Nick" himself laughing.

Anyway, your memory is remarkable. I don't blame you for carrying that handy little note-book and pencil around as a silent companion.

—— —— and myself went on a short trip to Miami, Florida. We found your letters when we returned, and lost no time in answering immediately.

It would be a pleasure to see you again. I sincerely hope that you will favor us with a visit at your earliest opportunity.

I must remember to add that your memory is a bit too painfully sharp in some spots. But, regardless, come again and I'll be too glad to supply more food for your articles in addition to what other political brothers have so kindly helped you with.

If, in writing your next article, you run short of incidents, let me know through mail, and I'll inform you with happenings *since you left*, that will fill a *whole magazine*.

Sincerely,

————— —————

DAVID NELSON

An Emperor Jones in Ward Politics

"But, Miss Merty, why d'you suppose I gave you the necklace?" This most natural question is found under a brilliant Peter Arno cartoon that appeared in *The New Yorker* for February 13, 1932. An irate though lovely lady, wearing a necklace of precious jewels, is about to smash a vase on an amazed society man who has just attempted to embrace her, the fair recipient of his earlier gift. He could not foresee a human nature so flexible that it would take a gentleman's diamond, but refuse his caress. If I were a Peter Arno I would do another cartoon suggested by recent talks with life-long politicians in Philadelphia. Many of these career men in politics are not only worried at the sight of 180,000 voters registering Democratic in a city that has not elected a Democratic Mayor since 1880, when Samuel G. King was chosen, but they are surprised and personally grieved to discover constituents to whom they had given tangible aid and comfort in the past, enrolled under the Democratic banner now. And although this feeling of disappointment is general throughout the ranks of the organization, it is found in its purest form among the leaders of the Afro-Americans.

Take the case of Handsome Dave Nelson. If Dave were not so big and substantial he might be a dandy. He is forty-five and looks younger. He is more than six feet tall and his carriage is good. There is a perceptible curve in front but no paunch. His clothes are tailored and he favors a dark brown suit with a herringbone stripe, with a fresh carnation in his lapel. (This carnation, like the big diamond on his left hand, is a badge of identity and is part of the man, just as Senator Salus's unlighted cigarette and Charlie Chaplin's moustache belong to these men.) His black pointed Oxfords never need a polish; an Italian bootblack in City Hall gives them a shine every morning—or noon, rather—when Dave appears there. His features are regular; his skin is ebony and his hair is black. His face is large and full; his even white teeth glisten when he smiles, and he smiles easily and often. I think that there must be a potential smile on his face even in repose, and when it breaks over his countenance as it does when he greets a friend, it is a cheery thing—something that makes one feel good. Dave is an Elk, and, while the bases of the strength of many politicians—particularly colored ones—are their lodge affiliations and their churches, it is not thus with Mr. Nelson. He is a Methodist, but in no sense a pillar of the church, not even a flying buttress. He says, "I don't go to church often, but neither do my people."

But one day when I saw him he had a puzzled, questioning look on his face. "A fellow came to me two years ago. He had consumption; he wanted to go to a hospital at Hamburg, Pennsylvania, but he couldn't get in. There was a waiting list. He tried for six months and then when he was pretty weak he came to me. I worked through Joe Blake [his assemblyman] and got

180

him right in. He was there a full year and came back stronger than I am. He said, 'Mr. Nelson, I'll never forget you.' Last week he registered Democratic. There are four in the family too. I saw him when he registered Democratic—he looked the other way. Hell, the only thing he could do for me was to register right; the only reason I did the favor was to get his vote.''

However, all of Dave's people are not consumptives; a winning majority have either gratitude or vision. Even the sleepy constituents heard the story of the number-writer who, when asked how he was going to vote in 1932, told Dave he was voting for Roosevelt. Dave did not argue, but a week later the writer was arrested for selling numbers (gambling slips). He called Dave on the telephone and begged for help. Dave calmly told him to get Roosevelt to speak to the magistrate in the case. "I help only Republicans." And this may explain why more than seven hundred of Dave's constituents registered Republican and less than one hundred Democratic, even in 1933 and 1934. The great majority of the people in this division are colored, but Dave serves them all—both black and white. "I always say 'Hello' to my neighbors and friends." (All the people living in his division are neighbors, and he probably has as many friends in City Hall as any division leader in Philadelphia.) He makes friends easily and, when he is seen once, he is never forgotten. He is an Emperor Jones in ward politics. His friends are part of the dividends that life pays him, and he works hard to maintain his prestige. He is so accommodating and so sure to produce results in a magistrate's court or a police station that sometimes voters from other divisions that feel skeptical of the ability of their own leader come to him. This activity on his part in behalf of individuals in distress that live outside his own precincts has won him the title of The National Committeeman. His colleagues protest against this extra-division activity, for they feel that it might undermine their own leadership. Dave says that all he is trying to do is to help the voter. To make this help certain he has a bell the size of a saucer rigged up beside his bed on the second floor. "When I go to bed I go to sleep and I could never hear the little bell downstairs. I got one now that wakes me up."

Saturday nights and Sundays are the busiest for Dave; every week-end fifteen or sixteen people come to get him to intercede for them—to say the one word to the politicians' tribune of justice, the magistrate. "I often get up at two or three in the morning to help get someone out of jail. In fact, I have to get up at this hour so regularly on Saturday nights that I never go to bed until 3 A.M."

Politics is Dave's first concern. "I like the life," he says; and dancing is his second love. He is a champion waltzer. He has won many prizes for the skill with which he and his lady waltz. He also used to give dances and dancing lessons. Now he is a mere devotee, but still ardent. He is not married; and when he goes to a dance, a problem is sure to arise. "I take my girl. The lady at the door says, 'There is a telephone call for you, Mr. Nelson.' The calls come so often that my girl gets sore." But although these interruptions are annoying, they are not serious, for Dave has a way with women.

182

DAVID NELSON

Mr. Nelson's parents were born in South Carolina. He was born in the XYZ Ward and lived there until he was twenty. Since then he has been living in his present ward. He is an only child; his father is dead and he lives with his mother. They live in a small frame two-story house on a corner. The outward appearance of the house is not markedly different from that of many of the others that line the narrow mean street that it faces, a street alive with colored people on a summer day—people squatting on their steps, or leaning out of an open window talking to someone in the street, or just gazing. The houses are forlorn looking, but the men, women, and children are not. As they lounge and sprawl and play about, they look contented and happy. They make one think of the Biblical passage about the lilies of the field. Mr. Nelson gets countless greetings as he swings down the small street of his domain. (The great majority of these constituents are colored, but there are eighty Jewish people in the division.) "All of them are for me!" says Dave; but, as an afterthought, "Woman suffrage makes politics different. In the past a man beat his wife and I would get him out. It made no difference about who was right. Now you got to keep the friendship of both. You must use your head to know who to help." It may be the record he has made or it may be his buoyant spirit, but, even in 1933, when the N.R.A. was knocking over leaders of more independent areas, Dave confidently expressed the conviction, "I'll never be beaten—not by human man or this inhuman N.R.A."

Nor do I speak lightly of Dave's claim. His ward is one of the first twenty; their tradition for voting regular

183

is a great one. They are the party's finest. The late leader of the tenth ward, Sunny Jim McNichol, once spoke for leaders and followers alike when he said, "A political party is like a great big family where leaders look after the wants of every member of the party like a father does his family. The members of a reform party never come around to do anything after election time."

Voting in this ward is more than a mere political act; it is hedged about with many of the social amenities. The ward is divided into divisions; there are two leaders or committeemen elected by the party voters in each division every two years. In a recent primary one of the division leaders distributed among his voters—both colored and white—a load of fish. Later in the day when these voters, many of them thirsty, came to the polls, they were provided with a drink. The vote that day was nearly unanimous. Regardless of race or creed, the voters in a slum ward think kindly of the politician that is thoughtful about the little things in life. "Blessed is the hand that gives." It was the same in the old days; and yet, according to one division leader "emeritus," it was different, too. In a long conversation at the historic ward club, he told me, "In the old days we would go to saloons and get delegates. No vote-buying —just a matter of treating. Today you have a class of people around here that are nothing. Vote-buying goes back to the Vare-Earle [1911] fight. Of course there are hangers-on that have always wanted money—but today it is almost a fixed thing that people want money. There are some very nice people in this ward to whom money

184

would be an insult, but the majority must be paid."
Later he added, "This ward has changed a lot. You
know, people that lived here long ago thought it was
wrong to take money for their vote. They thought it
was bribery." "What do they think it is now?" I asked.
"They think it is their duty to take money," was his
laconic reply. Dave, however, says that he frowns on
vote-buying, and he is trying to get his people away
from this practice, though fighting against the customs
of a neighborhood is uphill work. Dave's own position
on this subject of vote-buying with cash might be best
described by quoting a recent conversation with his
old friend, Tom Gibson. Tom said, "I once took my
coat and vest off to pay a fine, but I don't like to pay
them for votes. But you can't catch flies with vinegar.
I say to them, 'If you ask me for $2.00 or whatever you
get for your vote, all right, I'll pay you. But then you
are paid up, and then you can't come around during the
year for help.' Mr. Gibson emphasized this point. He preferred to serve the voter, but, if the voter demanded cash,
he could have cash. However, he could not have both.

"Suppose the man is paid for his vote and then in
three months or so, he gets locked up and sends for you,"
I asked. "Well," answered Tom, "I get him out of the
station house. Then a year later, election comes around
again, and he is very hard up and must be paid. So I give
him the cash at the next election too. But," and here
he opened his eyes wide and looked at me before proceed-
ing, "then he gets locked up again and sends for me.
This time I use my judgment. I tell them they can't have
both."

Once I met Dave as he was walking, in his rather lordly fashion, in the south corridor of the first floor of City Hall. He stopped to chat, but a car was circling City Hall waiting for him. One of his people was being held in a police station because his home had been raided, and liquor had been found; he had been arrested, and now Dave was going to obtain his release with a "copy of the charge," signed by a magistrate. He asked me to go along with him; we stopped long enough at the south entrance to buy a new carnation and discard the old one. A young colored boy, the son of the victim, was driving the car, an old Ford for which Dave apologized at great length.

At the station house Dave cheerfully spoke to the officers; the prisoner was turned over to him. All four of us drove around the corner to the shack-like structure in which the man lived. The prisoner and his political leader went inside the house for the final arrangements. While I was alone in the car three small colored children —all under six years of age—amused themselves by climbing into the front seat and sounding the horn.

When Dave appeared we walked to his own home, just three doors away. The house in which he lives is nondescript outwardly, but it is pleasing inside. There are four overstuffed chairs in the front room, which is long and narrow. There is also a sofa, and there are three huge photographs in ornate frames hanging on the walls, two likenesses of ancestors, and one of Paul Robeson.

Dave's mother, a surprisingly young-looking woman, was sitting in a chair by the window as we entered. She is a most fluent talker, and spoke with gusto about the number of people in distress who called to see her son, and "they come after we have gone to bed, too, and I got to wake Dave." (Presumably before the advent of the great bell.) She then walked to a room in the rear. After she had gone, Dave, comfortably seated in a morris chair and smoking a fine cigar, smiled broadly and said, "You ought to see Maizie Bilkins! She is a terror, but she is a friend of mine. She used to be a school teacher in New York. She sure can write wonderful when she is sober. I wish that I could write a hand like hers. Now she gets drunk for days at a time. When she gets arrested for raising Cain, I speak to the magistrate. She comes here a lot—she is either singing or crying or shouting. She's got an awful tongue. She tells it to them, no matter who! Maizie don't live any place—she just hangs around; she tells me what people say about me. If any opposition starts, I know it right soon. When I started living at Atlantic City for the summer, Maizie said to my mother, 'Sorry to see your son go to the shore. He's the only son of a bitch that can get me out if I'm locked up.' My mother had to laugh because Maizie is so serious. She is the best party worker I got—some people tell you one thing to your face, but they have a different story when you aren't there."

Dave has been in politics (which, in his case, is a combination of finance [low], Salvation Army work, and station-house fixing) for twenty-four years. He has always been popular, and, after being in the ward less than a year, he "took a hand" in the game of kings and gangsters. He was asked to help out in a primary, and has been helping out ever since. (His friends helped him

187

then, and they are the core of his strength now.) He sold newspapers while he was finishing grammar school. Next he operated an elevator, and then, for six years, he was an office boy for a state senator. After that he worked for the Pennsylvania railroad. But for the last ten years he has been on the public pay roll; his official work is not arduous—keeping ledgers in order—and his hours are not long. His official salary is $2,000, and he sometimes receives silver or gold from appreciative persons whom he has helped. The merit system that his job is under is a grueling one; it is the organization's own. His examinations come in the form of a direct primary and election, twice a year. So long as he passes these, *i.e.*, carries his division, his job is safe, budget-pruners, delinquent taxes, and the depression notwithstanding. But to pass these political tests he must nurse his constituency along nearly every day in the year. (When he is at the shore in the summer, he frequently comes home; and a young lieutenant takes care of his political work in the interims.)

On this day, at his home (September 15, 1933) he told me that he had helped four people within the last twenty-four hours. (1) He had secured the liberation of the man referred to above. (2) Two men and a woman, one a voter in the division, had been arrested for fighting on the street. (3) One of Dave's constituents had not received the life insurance carried by a brother that had recently died. (4) One far-sighted colored voter, seeing that a primary was only four days away and that his coal bin was empty, wanted Dave to assure him that he would have coal in time. Dave did not do anything definite about this, and laughed when he explained the man s request. These last twenty-four hours had brought less than the usual number of requests. The day before he had served ten individuals. In answer to another question, Dave emphatically said that 80 per cent of his political work consisted of station-house cases. He sighed for the early days, "when we could get jobs for everybody. We had a job in every house or so, and nobody was against us. Today the people fret around more." I well remember the answer that Dave's political mentor, Tom Gibson, gave to this question about service to voters when I asked him what other things he did for them. "There ain't nothing else. I don't know anything more you can do for a person than to feed them, buy them clothes, pay their rent, and bury them when they die. No sir, there ain't nothing else."

The subject changed; he commented on the difference between the problem confronting him and the leader of a West Philadelphia division. "Many of the people out there are home owners; here few own their homes, and my people are always on the move—here today and gone tomorrow! Then, my people do not have much education along this line. Some of them think that they are voting when they go to register. They say, 'Vote again! I just voted!' when they've only registered." Dave repeated a remark he had made good-naturedly to some leaders of independent districts who are holding nice jobs at City Hall. "Gee, you fellows get away with murder! You don't have to get anybody out of jail, or get jobs, or give away quarters!" (To vote in Philadelphia, one must be a property owner or pay 25 cents for a poll tax. In certain wards, including Dave's, this poll tax is paid by the committeemen. He would not permit a mere quarter to stand between him and a vote. Paying for poll taxes is one of the customs of the neighborhood.) This tax qualification for voting, however, has been legally abolished. But when I reminded him that he could carry his division in his vest pocket because his constituents had compelling wants, and he satisfied them, he agreed. A ward committeeman is the prototype of his people, and Dave is a tower of strength in his own community, where the people have desires and ambitions similar to his own, even though he would find himself altogether an outsider and of no importance in many districts of Germantown or West Philadelphia.

Dave was active in politics for sixteen years before he was elected to his ward committee. Finally, however, the negroes increased in such numbers that he felt—and mentioned the idea to some of his friends—that they ought to have representation on the ward committee. He had many white friends, too. One of them was the son of one of the two men on the committee. The father was old, about ready to retire. The son said, "I will help you if you promise to help me two years from now." The son worked for him and Dave won by four votes. (However, one of Dave's colored politician friends from a neighboring ward took a hand. He got Dave a watcher's certificate and Dave kept his eye on the ballot box until the votes were counted. Now there are a number of colored committeemen in this ward, but Dave was the first to break the ice.) At the next election, both the son of the former committeeman and Dave campaigned for office and both were elected. Since that time his ticket has never been defeated in the division.

190

Whenever vice—gambling, women, liquor—is strongly intrenched in a ward, election money is plentiful. A few years ago $1200 was spent in the division to beat Dave and his ward leader. Dave told his friends to take the money—which they did—and "stay with us." The opposition received 72 votes and Dave won with 330.

One of his workers in this contest was Dr. Trunker, "a fake doctor, goodest bull-shooter in the world. He got $250 to help the other side. He went around to every house in the neighborhood with a leader of the opposition. The leader would say why he was against me—the old colored doctor would agree to it, and then he would say to the people in the house as he was following the leader out, 'Don't pay any attention to that stuff,' and then to his employer, 'Come on, let's go next door.' Every night he would put a note under my door telling me who was against me.

"Then there was a colored minister. He came to my mother and said, 'Mrs. Nelson, they want me to go against your son. I would rather cut my arm off than go against him. Give me $1.00 for my church.'

"I saw him with the opposition. He whispered, 'Don't pay any attention to what you hear.'

"Later I called him a 'dirty crook.' The leader Judson heard me. He said to the minister, 'That don't sound so good. You are a man of God. Why don't you have him locked up for slander?'

"I said, 'Ask him about the time I got him out of jail.'

" 'Did he get you out for stealing?'

" 'No, not exactly that,' the minister said, 'Six years ago I was in the park. A man near me said that he was

191

robbed, and said I was doing it, but I was innocent as a lamb. But I was locked up, and Dave got me out.'

" 'Oh hell!' Judson said, 'You can't sue him for slander then!'

"One primary day a jack-leg minister (one without a church, you know—he preaches anywhere) came in to vote. I said, 'Are you a Republican or a Democrat?' He said, 'I'm a Baptist.' "

Once, in the midst of this long conversation at Dave's home, he laughed more loudly than usual, though whenever he tells about his experiences in politics, he laughs. "There used to be a Democratic leader in the division. He was the honestest fellow I know. You couldn't hire him for a $1,000,000. One day as his son came in to vote with a Democratic sample ballot that his father had given him, I quickly put a Republican ballot in its place. But the son discovered the trick before he went into the polling booth. He said, 'Father, I got a Republican ballot.' His father shouted at me, 'You dirty thief—you black scoundrel!' He was very mad but I only laughed. He was a good white fellow—I spent a couple of days getting somebody to get a mortgage for him, but he always worked against me until he moved."

As I was about to leave, Dave proudly showed me a picture of himself that had appeared in a local newspaper. Below the picture was his name and a news item informing the reader that Mr. David Nelson had won the Grand Prize for waltzing at the Annual Ball. The clipping was now carried in his large leather wallet. "I always keep this handy for identification purposes when I am away from home," he explained.

ROSIE POPOVITS

"She Is the Best Man on the Ward Committee"

➤➤

ROSIE POPOVITS is the successful leader of a division in one of the industrial wards of Philadelphia. She is so effective a politician that her ward leader once said that she was the best man on his ward committee. A knowing attorney in her ward commented: "She does very well in politics—even handling cases in the courts. Sometimes she can do things that men can't." Thirty-five years ago she was born in Austria; ten years later her family abandoned Europe for a greater life in America—they came directly to the industrial ward in Philadelphia where they now live. At that time she could speak German, Polish, Yiddish, and Russian, and she can speak three of these languages today, as well as English; this is one source of her strength in the "League of Nations" bailiwick that she claims as her own.

She is a cheery person to see, of medium height and fine stocky figure; there are curves where curves should be. Her face is a broad oval; her nose is Roman, and her forehead is not high; an abundance of chestnut hair is long and well cared for; her eyes are wide open and alert. Her mouth is generous in size, and, were it not for one gold tooth in front, it would be entirely prepossessing. As it is, her smile and her zest strike one first—and last.

And her European origin and ancestry have equipped her well for the rugged political life that she has entered. No habitué of City Hall or servant of the people relishes the atmosphere, the perennial discussions, or the give and take of politics more than Rosie. If she can carry her division of 658 voters in her vanity case, it is because she chooses to carry a man-sized load of neighborhood troubles on her back. She won her division in 1932 against Roosevelt, and in 1933 against a nebulous specter called the N.R.A., because she serves her people.

"I got into politics just on account of Mr. Shelden; also I like the work and am interested in helping the people—this is a poor neighborhood you know." (This simple explanation accounts for the presence of the great majority of organization leaders in politics. A friend wants them to help on some single occasion, and those that remain in politics after this initial venture keep on "helping" as long as life lasts.) Rosie's first taste of it was in 1922. Mr. Shelden was then the leader of the division. Mr. Paunock, his partner on the ward committee, lacked tact and energy and gave much of his time to the management of his trucking business. This left the burden of the political work on Mr. Shelden.

He was a personal friend of Rosie's father. He often dropped in for a friendly talk. The father is a laboring man not interested in politics, but he liked Mr. Shelden. Rosie's imagination was excited by the leader's endless fund of political folklore and his friendly attitude. In one of these innumerable talks he explained that his work at City Hall took so much of his time that he could not take care of the people. Rosie quickly volunteered to help. "He was a good friend of ours and I thought a lot of Mr. Shelden and said I would be more than glad to help him out. I went out among the neighbors and worked at the polls. Whatever he asked me to do I did; never took any money for it; always did it for Mr. Shelden and Mr. Griffiths [the ward leader], because he does a lot of good down here. Mr. Shelden told me, 'Rosie, anything that happens you take care of it.' Through them I had the preference of doing anything down here. I really do all the work down here. I got in between Mr. Shelden and Mr. Paunock. That was ten years ago in 1922. I am only 32 now; was 22 then. It was right after I cast my first vote!"

Mr. Shelden died a few years ago and Rosie was recognized by the ward leader ("Five years ago I never would have thought it possible," he said) as his successor; later she was officially elected to the ward committee at the primary. She has never held a position as an election official. "I just didn't want to be obligated; the assessor is Mr. Paunock's wife and I wouldn't want that job taken away from her. Neither did I want to be a watcher, for then, I would have to be inside and I have to be on the outside and bring the voters in."

Rosie married a dark and dapper Serb of twenty-one when she was nineteen. One can easily imagine her husband as an officer in the King's guards in some such exotic setting as is not infrequently provided by our Cecil De Milles. He looks the part and enjoys the favor his appearance brings him. They have a son of twelve and a daughter of seven. The children are unusually well mannered and handsome. One time I offered the little girl a nickel for ice cream; she smiled and refused the money until her mother nodded in approval.

This second child was born on the heels of an exciting election, but Rosie campaigned just the same. "I was never out of politics because of baby—worked at the polls in November—December I had my baby. People never knew that I had a baby; would say 'whose was that.' Big surprise to all of them. My mother lives across the street and she helped take care of my Anna when she was very young. I always take care of my home. [My several visits to her home support this statement. The home is small, comfortably furnished, and so far as a male could see, well cared for.] I am getting up at all hours of the night—whenever someone comes for me— and I get up in the morning at seven or eight. Probably a hearing [at a police station] in the morning. I get my kids' breakfast before that. I cook, wash my dishes, do everything myself in the house except wash. We can't afford to take someone in and keep them steady. We couldn't get along that way. We get along. We're happy. This is a pretty nice house." Later, in speaking of this phase of her life she added, "And I am never behind at home. I work hard but I like it. The people— the people—magistrate courts—City Hall. If I didn't enjoy every minute of the day I couldn't put up with it."

When I asked what there was to look forward to in politics, Rosie spoke from the heart. "What it is that keeps me—the truth is—when I married, my husband didn't make a very nice living—only a taxi-cab driver. I wanted him to get something better and I thought

I could get him in something better. I did. He is a police officer now. When I asked Mr. Shelden and Mr. Griffiths to do that I told them I wouldn't forget them. I feel it is my duty now."

The ward committee meets about eight times a year, but Rosie goes to only the most important meetings, those on the eve of an election. She does not want to be away when people call on her, and every evening someone is sure to come. However, she sees her leader nearly every day, and she skillfully manages to get along with him. She excels her partner on the ward committee in this respect. The day following the 1932 primary, for example, I was talking to the ward leader, Griffiths, in his office at City Hall. As we talked Mr. Paunock, Rosie's partner, came in. I greeted him with the query "How did you make out?" He smilingly answered, "I put up bail and walked out the other door." "Shut up, you fool," the ward leader exclaimed, "he means how did you do at the primary." Mr. Griffiths has strong points but tact is not one of them. In 1930 Paunock dropped in at his leader's office and held out his hand. The leader abruptly pointed to one of the other men in his office, and said, "Give it [the hand shake] to him; he saves them." This ungracious remark caused Paunock to buck the organization in the Pinchot-Hemphill election of that year. Paunock was able to bring Pinchot eleven votes; Rosie got the rest for the Democrat Hemphill.

Rosie takes care of her people as some mothers look after their children. One pleasant evening in June, 1932, I asked her to enumerate the demands that had been made on her during the last twenty-four hours. Each day is different, but the following record is descriptive of many days, not only in the life of Rosie, but in the life of the organization. (Not only the type, of course, but the degree of service in the 1,283 divisions varies as the cultural and economic planes of the people in the divisions vary. In this particular division, for example, the leader is ten or one hundred times as active as are certain leaders in more independent wards and divisions. The word "independent" means not only independent in politics, but independent economically, legally, intellectually, and with no language or tradition handicap.)

"I had one case this morning at eight o'clock. A man had an automobile accident with an officer. I had to go against my husband's brother—he is a policeman. The officer had him arrested which he shouldn't have done. He should have just taken his number and have him report. He brought him up to the station house and had him arrested and about a half an hour later he went back to the cell and let him out. Magistrate X is a very fine fellow. He discharged the case and called down the officer. Just because he is an officer doesn't mean he has the right to lock everybody up.

"There was another case about 11:30; boy arrested for bicycle accident—held for court under $300 bail. It was another boy that hit a boy in my division. The boy's mother is satisfied now that the boy has been taught a lesson."

At the primary Rosie's partner, Mr. Paunock, was arrested for assisting his wife (*i.e.*, marking her ballot). Rosie was "on this case" about five hours the preceding day, and today it came up in grand jury room 675. "It wasn't discharged before the magistrate because this magistrate isn't with us—Magistrate Carsons" (a magistrate appointed by Governor Pinchot, not elected by the organization). The fact that the case was discharged by the grand jury is descriptive of Rosie's influence rather than Paunock's.

Later that day Rosie called up the Lloyd Committee (welfare relief) to ask them to help a family in distress. "I have an engagement to take these people up. Miss X will take care of them for me. For three months they have had their application in and nothing has been done. I am going to find out why."

About 75 per cent of Rosie's work is concerned with magistrate cases. A voter is arrested, and Mrs. Popovits speaks to the "judge" for the voter in trouble. All twenty-eight of the magistrates are politicians and nearly all of them are either ward or division leaders. Their interest in a vote may be the same as that of a politician on the outside. There are exceptions, but this is the rule. She does not use attorneys. Many division leaders take cases to lawyers and in return receive 50 per cent of the fee. "I never send a voter to any attorney. You never know how it will turn out. They'll say you made some money on it. If anything afterward should happen they can't say anything to me. I can't annoy Mr. Griffiths for every little thing either."

The other 25 per cent of her time is devoted to social service or Salvation Army work of one sort or another, and to providing information concerning various taxes, licenses, and other governmental matters. The public importance of this work is so great to the citizens of Philadelphia that Rosie serves that she should be placed on the public pay roll without any make-believe job at City Hall.

In the 1932 primary the principal contest was between Pinchot's candidate, General Butler, and Vare's candidate, Senator Davis, the great Moose. The primary came on a Jewish holiday; only 350 people voted instead of the usual 425 to 530. A disgruntled Republican worked for Butler in the division and the General received forty-one votes. Rosie and Vare's candidate got the rest. She explained, "I wouldn't have had no argument here if I did like they wanted. The Butler people wanted me to give them seventy-five votes so that they could make a showing. I wouldn't do it. We had ten watchers [party workers] at $5.00. I had no women among the watchers. I could hire men and women but this time only men. It was sort of a hard fight and I thought I would do better that way. Two or three women came out anyway—just to give me a hand."

However, Rosie herself was a casualty in this senatorial campaign. One of Pinchot's workers standing in the polling place said that she assisted her husband in voting. Just as Mr. Popovits stepped into the polling place, Rosie spoke to him; told him, she says, to turn the fire down under the stew at home. "This fellow particularly was out to try to hurt us for he was a candidate for my place on the ward committee. He can't get it and he can't hurt me because I have no job, but a month ago he said he would get my husband's job.

200

I fought the case out myself and Magistrate X discharged it. They were trying hard to get me to sign papers that I'll keep away from politics. I said I work very hard in this division and I wouldn't care if it cost my husband's job. I wouldn't get out." And she has not gotten out. Mr. Shelden's last words to her were, "If I ever die don't step out; being a woman, go through with it."

Before I saw Mrs. Popovits again (nearly a year later), Mr. Paunock died. Rosie viewed the matter realistically and selected, as her partner, Frank Ricchino, a man of about thirty who enjoyed the distinction of being both a high-school graduate and a former professional heavyweight boxer. After working with him a while she said that the leadership in her bailiwick was stronger than ever and that, "Frank is there whenever I need a strong right arm, and his left is so good that he is called the Old Soak."

One day I was in a station house observing a magistrate pass on cases brought before him. The room was packed with loungers, spectators, friends of the accused, and those who had been summoned, as well as those in custody, officers, attorneys, politicians, clerks, and the magistrate. His Honor gave one, two, three, or four minutes to a case, and more defendants were dispatched in two than in four minutes. Instead of peaceful quiet or judicial calm, the atmosphere was one of rush, excitement, and hustle. Rosie walked into this room like an old trooper. She crawled under the rope—it is stretched across one end of the room to keep the idle public away from the prisoners—and straightway walked to a man acquaintance, spoke into his ear for

201

a minute; he nodded; she smiled, thanked him, and turned away. I joined her on the outside, and we boarded a trolley car going in the direction of City Hall. She explained that she had had a more compelling case at another station house, and she had asked the man to whom she had spoken, a division leader, to take care of her client at this court. And I found later that he had done as she had directed and all had been decided in her favor.

Although she said, "I got wonderful hopes in the organization. It can't be beat. It does too much good for the people," she too found September, 1933, a most trying time. For example, a man in her division who was working for the city as an auto mechanic had recently been demoted to a driver. "He makes a crack if Mr. Shelden had lived he would not have let them do that to me." Then there was the disloyalty of one of her watchers. "His family was starving last winter. I bought groceries out of my own pocket-book, then got them a welfare order of $6.50 a week. Got the order at once too. Now he is working against me." But the case that best revealed the ingratitude in man or the change in the temper of the people was one in which a man was arrested for selling liquor in a soda-water store. The place was padlocked as unsanitary. The proprietor broke into it and removed the equipment. He was arrested and held for a court trial. "I went his bail. I stayed in court and stood up as a character witness for him. I pleaded for a break. The judge gave it to him; six months parole was all he got. Now he is a Democratic watcher and gives me trouble. Argues

202

everything that I do. That is the experience we go through.''

Several months later I asked Rosie if she, as a ward politician, were confronted with any special disadvantages because of her sex. She said that there were certain difficulties on this score. Three lesser and rival politicians in the division tried to start a whispering campaign against her. The nub of the argument was ''I am a married woman, having two children, and my place was at home, and not at the polls.'' But though her enemies might say this about her, her constituents prefer, in the words of Omar, to ''take the cash and let the credit go.'' So long as she measurably satisfies their wants, they call Rosie ''Leader'' and let her manage her own family affairs.

John Tollagrata, the leader of a small anti-Vare faction in the division, sent word to Mr. Griffiths that, if the ward leader would replace Rosie with a man, then Tollagrata would return to the fold and bring his friends along. The leader told Mr. Tollagrata to go to hell and he told Rosie that so long as she kept up the good work he was 100 per cent behind her. She added with a smile, ''You see, that this so-called 'feminine charm' does not mean a thing in politics, and jealousy is the chief obstacle in a woman's path to success.'' Later she made an exception to this statement. ''Sometimes when I appear before a magistrate with a 'copy of the charge' he grants my request and frees the prisoner although he has never seen me before. This does not happen often, and when it does happen, the judge is a gentleman, and he wants to extend a courtesy to a lady.''

203

Mrs. Popovits was particularly active in the primary and election periods of this year. The American voter invariably follows the rule formulated in the Book of Ecclesiastes. "In the day of prosperity be joyful; and in the day of adversity consider." Rosie's voters were considering, and she and the most powerful of the other 2,559 ward committeemen were answering these considerations, not with words, but with services. But in certain wards, including Rosie's, democracy is handicapped by the astigmatism of the voters. This is an advantage to the active division leader, for he comes right down where the voter lives, and he trades a concrete favor or a smile for a vote. One of the more intelligent of Rosie's people said, "We are too poor to enjoy the luxury of a protest vote. The vote to me is like a pay check. I get something for it."

Just before the primary a man and his wife were arrested in Rosie's division for operating a disorderly house. At the raid five girls and eight men were arrested. The police obtained from the girls a record of the number of men that they served each night and the sum of money each man paid. The police identified one of the men as a white slaver. The magistrate held all the defendants for court. The testimony at the trial brought out the fact that the girls met the men in a certain room on the second floor. (There are only two rooms upstairs.) The other room was used as a bedroom by the three children of the accused. "I pleaded for her but it didn't help."

Rosie's attitude in this case is the authentic attitude of those Americans who say, "May my country ever be right, but right or wrong my country, my party,

204

and here, my voter." Rosie and the great majority of party workers in Philadelphia think of themselves as "good people," as angels of mercy, as emissaries of the Lord as well as of Vare. In situations of this sort that shock the sensibilities of a gentle person, Rosie's full attention is fixed on her voter in distress—the city of Philadelphia is not even a phantom figure on the rim of her mind. Truth and justice may be as strong as one thousand men in some places, but not at the polls. The party worker is thinking of majorities. So long as there are neighborhoods where helping a white slaver is a popular act, the professional politician will help him. Down in these nerve cells—*i.e.*, divisions—of the city, the politician that survives year after year is a prototype of his people.

(The Republican party is not only a different thing to different men, but it is one thing in one ward and something different in another type of ward area even in the same city. Furthermore, the GOP in Pennsylvania is not the GOP in Wisconsin. And in Philadelphia a vote-winning act in the Tenth Ward on the part of a division leader might lead to social and political ostracism in the independent Germantown sector of the Twenty-second Ward. It is because Americans generally and in normal times are not so much interested in ideas and intangible values as they are in goods and services that Vare's organization and Tammany Hall continue—with rare exceptions like 1933—to win victories, and that men who rely on logic in a campaign are usually defeated. I can count on the fingers of one hand those politicians out of the several hundred to whom I have talked, who have been bothered by their consciences. If they think about the matter at all, they probably say with Bates in King Henry's army: "We know enough if we know we are the king's subject; if his cause be wrong, our obedience to the king wipes the crime of it out of us.")

Once while talking to Mrs. Popovits at her home I asked if she did not often find herself at odds with her husband because of his work as an officer of the law. She replied, "My husband is in another neighborhood. He does not bother about my affairs and I never ask him about his. Whatever he does is all right with me and what I do is all right with him. We are very broad-minded."

A few minutes later, the dapper Mr. Popovits came home. He started right in. "When we got married she didn't know anything about politics. Mr. Shelden asked me if my wife could give him a lift now and then. She got one hundred more votes than Paunock. Everyone knew her up at the Hall. She worked a long time before she got on the ward committee. Griffiths wanted her. But there is a strong prejudice against women. I am friendly with everybody on the beat. I arrested Spiffy. Told him, 'Now I suppose you must get your committee-man.' He said, 'I ain't got no committeeman, I got a committeewoman.' 'Who is she?' 'Rosie Popovits.' Was I surprised? But politics ain't no good. Christmas and New Year we have the house full of baskets. No one pays for it, only me."

At this Rosie tartly said, "Now, Mr. Popovits, you pay attention to your own affairs and leave politics

206

to me." But he took a last fling, "Since we have been in politics, we owe $1000—all politics."

After the 1933 election Rosie said, "It was a tough day for me, but I was rewarded. I carried my division. Mr. Griffiths carried the ward, but the battle in many of the other wards was lost. But I have already started working for a victory in 1934." And she won in 1934, too. It was "the meanest election ever held."

A drop of blood under a microscope may reveal the state of the patient's blood stream. Similarly, a close examination of one ward politician in action might be descriptive of ward politics generally. In either case, the evidence is entirely meaningful only when other factors are taken into consideration. As for the patient, was he at rest or in action; was he in health or in illness; was the blood freely given or taken by force? As for Rosie, I can say that she knew me before I knew her, and that she talked freely and with spontaneity. She thinks that the work she is doing is important, and she is pleased that a professor thinks so, too. She is a woman in politics, and her life on the ward committee is based on the fact that she is *regular*, not *independent*, and effectively serves her people. The fact of her sex is significant in some relations certainly, but it is dwarfed by other factors in politics. What she is and what she does depends less on sex than on her own attitude and the social, economic, and cultural conditions under which she lives. And this I think is largely true of all people in politics whether they be men or women.

III
DEFEAT:
NOVEMBER 7, 1933

•

Defeat: November 7, 1933

>>>->>>->>>->>>->>>->>>->>>->>>->>>->>>->>>(((-(((-(((-(((-(((-(((-(((-(((-(((-(((-(((

PHILADELPHIA was founded in 1682–1683. Its first charter was granted by William Penn in 1701; its present charter was a gift from Boies Penrose in 1919. (Senator Penrose bestowed a modern charter on Philadelphia in order to handicap his troublesome rivals in Philadelphia politics, the Vares.) From earliest times until the present the government of this imperial city has been more truly articulated with a leader or boss and his unofficial organization, than with public officials provided for by the charter. According to Colonel John Irving Dillon, nine bosses or feudal barons have ruled Philadelphia for the last eighty-four years—William B. Mann, Robert Mackey, James M'Manes, David Martin, Isreal Durham, Boies Penrose, Edwin H. Vare, and William S. Vare. They were the government that ran the government, the inevitable human equation functioning in the urban democratic community.

Philadelphia may be characterized by such terms as "an imperial air," "a tolerant attitude," and "a cold eye." It, moreover, never has been a rebel city. From earliest times it has favored the regular organization rather than the insurgents. When Washington's army, one bitter winter, was poorly fed—if fed at all—at

Valley Forge, the chosen of the British were eating of the best in Philadelphia. Beard quotes a colonial Democrat living there in 1776 as saying. "A poor man has rarely the honor of speaking to a gentleman on any terms and never with any familiarity but for a few weeks before the election. . . . Be freemen then, and you will be companions for gentlemen annually." This idea has carried over from that day, save that now this last statement should read, "Vote the organization ticket and you will be companions for politicians whenever you see them."

Although Philadelphia is an organization city, it is also the home of many courageous and capable independent leaders—individuals of unquestioned integrity and vision. This group, plus warring factional leaders within the organization, have enabled the city from time to time to overcome the boss, and to elect antiorganization candidates. The history of Philadelphia politics might almost as truly be written in terms of Committees of One Hundred, Town Meeting parties, and other independent groups as in terms of the Republican organization, save that the latter more often wins, and the independent groups never win twice in succession. Politics are too much bother for all but politicians except in times of stress and tension, as for example in 1881, or in 1905, when the organization was defeated because of the publicity given to the affairs of a mismanaged city; or in 1911, when it was defeated because of the appeal of Blankenburg and the split between the Penrose and Vare factions; or in 1933, when the depression plus the inadequate leadership of the party led to its latest defeat. The purpose of this chapter is to describe more fully this new balance of power that resulted in a Democratic victory.

"In the day of prosperity be joyful, and in the day of adversity consider." This injunction from Ecclesiastes has probably been more faithfully observed by the American voter than any other exhortation in the Bible. It goes far to explain the strength of the municipal boss during the long normal periods since the Civil War, and his overwhelming defeat in a depression. "Hard times" are against the party in power: they inevitably generate a wave of sentiment and opinion that engulf all that stand before them. The "ins" are washed out, and the "outs," no matter who they may be, are carried in. The *Zeitgeist* here is the controlling factor; the personal fortunes of a candidate may be enhanced or retarded by factors over which he has no control. For notwithstanding all that ward politicians do in normal times to serve their voters, a depression of such proportions as we have had reaches employer and employee in every commercial enterprise, so that no one can help feeling that something is very much wrong, and nearly everybody is inevitably propelled by the urge that insistently calls for a change. This state of mind was the first big factor in the Vare organization's defeat; and then from the moment that Franklin D. Roosevelt became President, and provided the country with dynamic leadership, the blind desire for change was transformed into a positive desire to support his New Deal program. In this growing tide of sentiment

213

the Philadelphia voter, whether he was day laborer or business man, turned to the Democratic party along with the rest of the country.

Moreover, not only did the depression affect the garden variety of voter beyond the power of the organization to make it up to him, but the organization itself had gone through such an acute depression in its own innermost structure that the jobs and funds normally available to party workers seemed to be drawn away right when they were most needed. The traditional aids and comforts (save the magistrate courts, which do as much business—*i.e.*, serve the organization—in a depression as in times of plenty) of the organization shrank away from the ultimate voter and from the ward committeeman, who is usually equipped to hold that voter in line, right at a time when the Republican party was facing its stiffest engagement within the memory of man.

The Republican party was not prepared for a hard campaign. It was weak when it should have been strong. William S. Vare suffered a paralytic stroke in August, 1928, and after that time the party was guided by an absentee leader. This weakened the morale of politician and voter. A political group may survive with a dying leader in peace times, but in war some commanding figure must take the field against the enemy.

The Republican party has ruled Philadelphia for a generation without any opposing party to discipline it, and since the death of Penrose in 1921 there has been no powerful opposition to the Vare leadership within the party. Under these circumstances it was inevitable that

214

the dominant group, were it not checked, would accumulate dry rot and engender enough poison to kill itself. The Russians attempt to obviate a condition like this. They, too, are ruled by one party and they have created an institution known as the "party purge" to keep the all-powerful Communist party of the Soviet Union free from cancerous growths. According to W. H. Chamberlain, the Control Commission acting through a network of local commissions excludes over 2 per cent of the members of the party every year. Party expulsion is the result of any serious shortcoming in thought or action on the part of the member, such as drunkenness, holding heretical political views, or disregard for the common good (as Communists define the common good). At longer intervals there are wholesale party purges, when each member must publicly stand before party judges and confess both his virtues and his weaknesses. It is, as Eugene Lyons recently remarked, "a confessional more searching and soul-searing than any ordained by older faiths—a confessional in which there is never any privileged secrecy and rarely any absolution; in which punishment is not deferred to a hereafter but is meted out on the spot." In the January, 1934, purging, possibly as many as 600,000 Communists were forced out of the party. However, it is plainly evident that this institution is as foreign to Philadelphia and the tolerant Republican party as the great Russian bear is to the woods and fields of Fairmount Park.

The uncertain leadership of the party in Philadelphia created opposition within its own ranks and was another indication of the party's need of purging. Governor

Pinchot provided patronage for anti-Vare workers, and Harry A. Mackey, a former Mayor who tried, in a revolt in 1929, to take Vare's toga when the leader was ill, and failed, and who, off and on, since that time has been outside the pale, campaigned for the Democrats and independent Republicans who were organized in a newly preempted Town Meeting Party. This latter group supplied only about 35,000 votes, however, and since the opposition vote was more than twice this large the election resulted in a Democratic rather than a fusion victory.

Plus all this, until 1933 the Democratic party in Philadelphia had been a fake; it was a section of the Republican organization that campaigned under the Democratic label in order to obtain minority positions. The chairman of its official City Committee (John O'Donnell) was as loyal to Vare as any of the Republican ward leaders. In return Vare permitted him to be the County Commissioner of the minority party.

Now under the stimulus of what was happening at Washington in 1933, a real Democratic party got under way. This group of anti-Vare Democrats were powerfully aided in their new role by a vigorous, liberal, and crusading newspaper—the *Philadelphia Record*, published by J. David Stern. Mr. Stern is a real power among the Democrats today although the handsome John B. Kelly, former champion oarsman, is the official chairman of the newly reorganized Democratic City Committee. This group defeated O'Donnell's nominees in the September primary and they were further strengthened by Farley's Federal patronage. And while the old Demo-

216

cratic party failed even to irritate the Republicans, this new Democratic party encompassed their defeat.

The Depression

To understand the significance of the economic factor in the recent Philadelphia election one might advantageously reexamine what happened nationally in the preceding year. Economic adversity was the biggest single reason why in 1932 the Democratic candidate for the Presidency carried 42 states, why Democratic candidates for the United States Senate won 27 places and lost 5, why 313 out of 435 congressional districts elected Democratic Congressmen, and why 30 states out of 35 chose Democratic governors.

The interest in this great Democratic victory is heightened when one realizes that it occurred in a country in which the Republicans in presidential elections and in many state elections not only have a well-defined tradition of winning, but normally possess a majority of the voters, the public jobs, the newspapers, and the greater war chest. However, the Grand Old Party fell to pieces like a worn-out garment in face of the mandate from the people.

In 1932 Pennsylvania had been one of the few states in which the *Literary Digest's* poll missed fire; Hoover carried the Keystone state, but by a fraction of its usual majorities, and he won Philadelphia by 70,716 votes, while Coolidge in 1924 had won by 293,244 votes over John Davis. In 1933, 178,870 citizens registered Democratic; never before in Philadelphia's history had this happened. The Democratic registration is usually much less than 85,000 (85,000 all told and a real percentage of these voters are Republicans who register Democratic to accommodate their Republican leader); and, moreover, from the organization politician's standpoint, these registration figures told only half of the story. Other thousands who were afraid to register publicly their protest, intended, unless they were watched or "assisted," to vote Democratic in November. An apprehension of something like this was the feeling I noticed in September, 1933, as I talked to some of the "regulars" in City Hall. These organization leaders were worried as they had not been since the revolution of 1905. The tension in organization circles was increased by the feeling that their opposition was not a person but an idea—"Democracy is in the air. The people don't know what they are doing. They are suffering from the depression and are going toward the Democratic party like an ocean tide. They have forgotten the years in which the Republican party has befriended them."

The organization won the primary, but the majorities were reduced and three old-time ward leaders worked against the Vare slate. In addition WillB. Hadley and S. Davis Wilson, anti-organization candidates for the important offices of City Treasurer and City Controller, contended for both the Republican and Democratic nominations. They won the Democratic nominations, and, wha twas more significant, their combined vote on both tickets exceeded the total vote of the Republican nominees.

In the November 7, 1933, election the voter might well have become confused at his task, for he was confronted with 1,942 square inches of ballot—the largest of the three ballots was 36 inches long and 19¼ inches wide. According to the *Evening Bulletin* these were the largest ballots ever used in Philadelphia's history. Twenty-four of the fifty wards used voting machines, and the voters in these wards were provided with an extra paper ballot. The elector was asked to choose: five common pleas court judges, six municipal court judges, sixteen magistrates (out of twenty-eight), a register of wills, city treasurer, city controller, and a coroner, as well as election officers, and assessors in the 1,280 divisions. Constables and poor-board members in special districts were also to be chosen at this time. In addition the electorate was asked to vote upon twelve proposed amendments to the Pennsylvania Constitution and a referendum on Sunday football, and to elect fifteen delegates at large to a convention for ratifying or rejecting the Twenty-first Amendment to the Federal Constitution. Questions confronting the voter were so numerous that, according to the logical reasoning of the advocates of the short ballot, this represented, not one single election, but fifty or more elections rolled into one. However, in spite of this monster ballot, the Philadelphia voter did express his mind that day, in no uncertain Democratic terms.

Napoleon said thàt God is on the side of the biggest armies; and the smallest Napoleon in politics knows that God, or a controlling number of voters, is invariably on the side of the strongest party organizations. But although this statement explains nineteen elections out of twenty in densely populated areas, it does not help one understand the electoral results of a 1932 or 1933.

To understand the defeat of party organizations accustomed to victory, one needs to ponder the above quoted statement from the Book of Ecclesiastes, or the observation of the father of modern political science, "Men do sooner forget the death of their father than the loss of their patrimony." These pertinent observations are as descriptive of Americans today as the former was of Chaldeans in the fourth century B. C. and the latter was of Florentines in 1513.

It is only depressions or catastrophes that can, as a rule, generate enough energy to arouse the people out of their lethargy, indifference, or traditional way of voting. In 1900 a tidal wave that destroyed seven thousand lives and $20,000,000 of property in Galveston led to the introduction of the commission plan of government in that city, and thirteen years later the flood of the Miami River led Dayton to adopt the city-manager plan. As for Cincinnati, Murray Seasongood writes, "It appears to be regrettably true that things must be very bad before they can begin to be good." Conditions became so bad there under the absentee leadership of Hynicka that the people voted for a complete change in 1925 without first suffering fire, earthquake, or flood. And in like manner, depressions are invariably hostile to the political party in power and can effect a reform where mere revelations of corruption fail. Any economic maladjustment is sure to be a tremendously powerful agent for change, and a general house cleaning. Corruption—even such colossal corruption as was discovered under the Republicans during Harding's regime—was not enough to turn the GOP out of power; and revealed

220

corruption among the Democrats in New York City under Mayor Walker at first caused smiles as well as frowns. At some of those public hearings Seabury, not Walker, was hissed. But the electorate is less tolerant of public dishonesty and wastefulness in times of economic distress. When this most sensitive pocket-book nerve is touched, as it has been in the United States since 1929, the voter is pricked to action and he votes against the party in power. At first it is more a "vote against" somebody, than a "vote for" some particular candidates. It is one time when public opinion speaks with a finality that cannot be ignored.

The awakening of the Philadelphia taxpayer through the effects of the depression upon his pocket-book, and his resultant demands for economy caused a change in division lines that was a decided handicap to politicians working for the Republican party. In 1932 Philadelphia comprised 1,566 divisions, but owing to original inequalities and the differences in growth of population these divisions were unequal in size. As an economy move they accordingly were reduced to 1,280* in number before the 1933 primary. This move struck at the backbone of the ward committeeman's strength. Changing the boundaries of division lines meant that the leader was confronted with new faces in his bailiwick. There was not enough time for him to establish the same sort of friendly relations with the new constituents that he already had with the old. The problem of carrying divisions was consequently more difficult and in many cases impossible. It would be very much like changing

* The number of divisions has since been increased to 1,283.

the boundary lines of Pennsylvania so as to include a portion of New Jersey or Ohio, or changing Senator Borah's Idaho to include a section of Montana. No one can doubt that the state politicians in either Pennsylvania or Idaho would most strenuously object. Their problem of reelection would have an element of uncertainty in it not to their liking. Furthermore, just as the reduction in the number of divisions handicapped the organization, it materially helped the anti-organization groups, the new Democratic and Town Meeting parties. With fewer divisions the opposition could more easily organize and with fewer workers man the polls—a condition to be desired by a disinterested person.

The atmosphere was so charged with the New Deal, Roosevelt democracy, and resentment against the Vare leadership that the anti-organization groups manned the polls, stood guard over the ballot boxes, and watched the voting in a most effective fashion. And because this ubiquitous opposition worker was real, and would not sell out, or could not be frightened away, the chances for fraudulent voting were correspondingly reduced. There was less fraud and strong-arm work in Philadelphia on November 7, 1933, than in any previous election in recent years. This was solely because the opposition was effectively organized to prevent it. A ballot-box artist in a ward so favorable to the exercise of his special talent that it produces more phantom voters per square foot than any other, said that the chances for stealing in this 1933 election were nil. He tried it and was stopped for the first time in his life.

Up to now he had not known that the law reached down where he lives. And as his ward is one of the few bad spots in the city, his experience shows the way the wind was blowing.

Another practice that sometimes reduces voting to less than a form is technically called "assistance to voters." That is, the division leader, or his representative, marks the ballot for the theoretically incapacitated person and then the theoretical voter drops the ballot into the box (see page 149). Divisions, in which three hundred out of three hundred voters had been assisted in 1930, 1931, and before, assisted fewer than thirty people in November, 1933. Of course, there were exceptions, and there were warrants issued and arrests made for poll violations, illegal assistance, intimidation, and violence, as well as for fraudulent registration. But with one hundred attorneys provided by the Democratic Campaign Committee ready at telephones to answer calls concerning ballot frauds, and with wide-awake opposition in the different polling places, and with the garden variety of elector more than ever interested in the free exercise of his franchise, Philadelphia approached a free election.

As a further result of this new spirit at the election, and of genuine significance for the future, is the fact that the Democrats captured the election machinery in many divisions, probably more than half the 1,280 in the city. Heretofore the Republican organization has reenforced its strength by electing, in the great majority of wards, its "own" election officials. This, of course, means that the judge of the election and the two inspectors could usually be counted upon to favor the organization in deciding questions arising out of the process of voting. And in certain wards and in normal elections the cooperation of the so-called officials meant extra votes in the ballot box regardless of the issues or candidates. But the Democratic tide upset this arrangement in an unprecedented fashion. And the loss of the election judge and inspectors has caused, and probably will continue to cause, the division worker in politics more sorrow than would the loss of a President or a governor.

The Philadelphia organization, like any other particularly powerful party organization, is a service institution; and service means favors—jobs for the party workers and material benefits of a sort for some of the needy among the electorate, as well as different concessions for utilities and other commercial enterprises. "The wheel that squeaks loudest gets the most grease," is a saying descriptive of the trend of political favors, but if there are more wheels squeaking than there is grease to satisfy them, a reaction sets in. This is what happened in 1933 and in 1932. Last year many party workers, including leaders of divisions, were deprived of public office, and an even greater number had their pay reduced. Such a reduction is bound to generate ill will. The resentment of many workers over the loss of their jobs or the reduction in their pay was intensified by a feeling that some powerful vote-producers were laid off, while other less successful ones remained because they enjoyed the friendship or kinship of some prince of the party. Knowledge of instances of this sort engendered a feeling that led some committeemen to work for the opposition, and others to do less than their best in working for the organization. Furthermore, the party worker was not able materially to help his constituents as he had done in the past; when some of them had too little for themselves, they could not help others. This led increasing numbers of people to turn from their division leader in their need to the party of President Roosevelt and the New Deal. And it led Republican leaders, in various sections of the city to do the same thing. They and their voters broke loyalties of many years standing, and climbed on the band wagon together.

Since the advent of Mayor J. Hampton Moore in January, 1932, expenditures had been held down. No unusual extravagances were revealed during this period save petty wastes under the Fairmount Park Commission, and petty graft in certain poor-board districts which are not under the control of the Mayor. In the budget for 1932, City Council reduced the pay of all city and county employees, receiving more than $1,200 a year by 10 per cent, although policemen, firemen, park guards, and several other groups of protective workers were excepted from this cut at first. In addition, many of the appropriations for personal service were reduced to only 84 per cent of the amounts needed to pay the reduced rates, making necessary still further pay-roll retrenchment. This was achieved through vacations without pay and staggering employment lay-offs; 2,350 persons under the Civil Service Commission were dropped from the pay roll between November 30, 1931, and December 31, 1932. There were minor reductions in the county

225

departments also, where the test for office is the ability to carry a division; this domain the civil-service regulations do not reach even in name, but the retrenchments reached there—enough to irritate the organization's finest.

In 1933 the pay of public employees was still further reduced. Salaried employees were forced to take a cut of 23 per cent of their annual pay over $600. Per diem employees were forced to take a cut of 25 per cent of the excess of their pay over $2.00 a day. There were also further reductions in the number of persons on the pay roll in 1933, although I do not have the exact figures. The dissatisfaction caused among organization workers by these economies, lost, in the organization, far more votes through resentment engendered among division workers than it gained through satisfying a general public demand. Thus the organization had failed to take care of its own, and was still less able materially to improve the conditions created by unemployment—both factors weakening the morale of the party workers. The politician is loyal because he wants security, but in 1933 there was no security in the organization ranks. Hence the feeling was strengthened that Vare's days were at an end—President Roosevelt was the man of the hour.

Although there were fewer unemployed persons in Philadelphia on November 15, 1933, than on December 15, 1932, the difference was too slight to counteract the drift of opinion that was forming against the organization. According to the reports on unemployment in Philadelphia by the Industrial Research Department of the University of Pennsylvania, the number of totally

226

unemployed persons on November 15, 1933, was 276,000, or 30.3 per cent of the usually gainfully employed population. This is an improvement over conditions on December 15, 1932, when 84,000 additional persons were totally unemployed. But it did not register as an improvement because there were still too many people out of work, and with a figure on the horizon as promising as Franklin D. Roosevelt the voters eagerly turned toward what they hoped would be a New Deal for them. Roosevelt did for the local Democrats what Abraham Lincoln has done countless times for local Republicans— provided a ticket with a glamour greater than that inspired by any of its candidates.

But the cumulative discontent with existing organizations and conditions was, as I have said, overwhelmingly expressed at the presidential election, and it has not exhausted itself yet. How long it will last no man can say. It nearly put Philadelphia in the Democratic column in 1934, when Pennsylvania elected a Democratic governor and United States Senator. The future popularity of President Roosevelt and the caliber of Democratic and Republican candidates in coming campaigns will bear in an important manner on this question, not only in Philadelphia but elsewhere. It is interesting to note that Governor Phil LaFollette was defeated for reelection in 1932 because of the depression; however, in 1934 LaFollette was reelected Governor on a Progressive ticket, defeating Governor Al Schmedeman, a Democrat. The voters in Wisconsin were evidently of the opinion that the Progressive LaFollettes were more apt to act in harmony with the spirit of Roosevelt's

227

program than would the Democratic Schmedeman. And in connection with the Progressive Victory in Wisconsin, it should be noted that their party organization is as superior to the Democratic organization in Wisconsin as a modern streamline automobile is superior to a horse and buggy for "going places" quickly. Moreover, the Progressive politicians have had an unusual amount of experience in educating the voters in political campaigns, and their leaders are men of exceptional ability.

Weakness in Leadership

The attitude of restlessness which played so large a part in the Philadelphia election was by no means confined to Philadelphia; it was common to other cities, New York, Pittsburgh, Bridgeport, and Scranton, as well as Philadelphia; but in Philadelphia it was especially significant. And of course there were many contributing factors in the defeat, and some especially strong ones in the case of Philadelphia.

First to be noted among these factors were the blunders of the Vare leadership. As I have said, the leader, William S. Vare, suffered a paralytic stroke in August, 1928. From then on Philadelphia had been governed by absentee leadership, for Vare had remained in either Atlantic City or St. Lucie, Florida. Up until 1931 he would come to his Philadelphia offices for an hour or two on several days a week, but he gradually became too weak physically to do even that. After the warning registered in the September, 1933, primary, however, he took the field in person (from a bed) and moved to the Warwick Hotel in Philadelphia. This might have

228

helped more had his brain been as keen as it had once been, but it was not. He was forced to rely increasingly on advisers; and in selecting them he was guided by Grand Duke Alexander's comment that a minister's loyalty to the throne may be worth more than his talents. Vare's central thought was to confer with loyal counselors. This led him to ignore the advice of some of the organization's keenest thinkers.

Vare, guided by a synthetic leadership, made an inexcusable mistake in slating the vulnerable Edward Merchant, Secretary of the Board of Public Education, for the important place of City Controller. Before the primary campaign was well under way, an organization apostate, Benjamin M. Golder, publicly charged Merchant with various irregularities in the purchase of real estate for the Board of Public Education. (In 1932 Congressman Golder had been denied renomination to Congress, and he had thereupon waged against Vare and the Vare leaders in his own district a campaign of bitter and vitriolic charges that had led Mr. Sellers [Vare's nominee] to commit suicide shortly after he had won the nomination.)

Vare's blunder in slating Merchant at any time, but especially at a critical time, with the effective campaigner Golder watching the horizon for something to attack, was doubly bad; Merchant's transactions in the Board of Education were known by enough people so that Vare could not plead ignorance. Vare was warned against this nomination by clear-headed members of the organization, but their protests were curtly dismissed.

The Board of Education appointed an investigating committee, and the newspapers carried solid pages of the testimony for a number of weeks, and the *Record*, in particular, published much invective in its editorial columns against Merchant. Though he finally won the nomination, the organization, after the primary, substituted a respectable attorney, Chester N. Farr, a man of high standing, in his place. Unfortunately for the organization, however, Mr. Farr was also a member of the Board of Public Education, and the trend of sentiment against the organization and the revealed carelessness and extravagances of the school board could not be stopped. Mr. Farr lost the election.

A second blunder was that Vare sponsored an exchange of important county offices between two old-time ward leaders, Register of Wills Billy Campbell and Coroner Fred Schwartz. They are both colorful men, but in 1933 the electorate was more interested in real ability than color. Furthermore Mr. Campbell was just finishing his third four-year term in this most lucrative office, and switching him over to the Coroner's office, or the other life-long placeholder to the Register of Wills office, awakened no enthusiasm save in the two men concerned, and angered and incensed many organization followers who thought that someone else should have been given a chance. This particular move, along with sacrificing a certain amount of good will within the organization, did nothing to awaken confidence in the voters generally.

Vare's next mistake can best be explained by the deadening effect of his paralytic stroke, for, in tampering with the municipal court in a critical 1933, he did what no boss with all his normal faculties would ever have done—attempted to replace several judges with men of unquestioned loyalty to him. Even though one of the shrewdest politicians in Philadelphia is a judge; though several other judges are the real leaders of wards, in actuality if not in name; though still others are powerful vote-getters; and the popular President Judge of the Common Pleas Court, No. 1, Harry S. McDevitt, has been mentioned in the newspapers as a possible successor to Vare—yet, Philadelphia likes to think of the judiciary as apart from politics, and favors the retention of sitting jurists unless there is some particular reason why they should not stay on the bench. In spite of this attitude of the electorate, which is tantamount to a tradition, Vare attempted to make over the municipal court.

At first it was rumored that he was going to refuse to support William M. Lewis for reelection. However, the protests that came to him and his high council were significant enough to convert him to Judge Lewis. But much of the damage had been done and the sentinels of the people were wary. Before the primary election the tocsins were sounded to save the courts from the organization's raid.

Then Vare refused his endorsement to Judge Utley E. Crane because he was personally friendly to the leader's enemy, the former Mayor, Harry Mackey. Judge Crane had won the approval of the Philadelphia attorneys by a very large majority in a special primary held by the Bar Association and was generally well thought of. The leader also refused to endorse Eugene C. Bonniwell for renomination. This time he acted in harmony with

231

the positive expression of disapproval registered in the Bar Association primary. However, Vare opposed Bonniwell because the jurist had campaigned for Gifford Pinchot and could not be relied on as a Vare order-taker. The attorneys opposed his retention on the bench because he was not, in their estimation, a worthy man for the judicial office. Nevertheless, Bonniwell is known, has friends, and is a tower of strength in certain Catholic organizations and sporting groups. One ward leader said that the organization lost thirty thousand votes right here, and possibly twice that many. In any event the electorate reelected all sitting judges.

In addition Vare opposed the nomination and election of Judge Albert S. C. Millar of Common Pleas Court, No. 3. (The Bar Association primary also voted 353 to 178 against recommending him to the office to which he had been appointed by Governor Pinchot.) Vare sponsored his personal legal counsel, Edward A. Kelly, for the place. Millar won the election by more than sixty thousand votes.

"The reason we lost the election was they gave us a nigger instead of a shine." (The two words *nigger* and *shine* imply a social distinction.) This is the personal explanation of the organization's defeat that one ward leader gave to a friend a few days after the election. He was referring to Vare's refusal to slate Magistrate Edward W. Henry, a negro, but not a Vare man, for another term as magistrate. In his place, instead of making a bid for Henry's support, which he could have had, he proposed to substitute a colored stalwart, John C. Asbury, for the position. Mr. Asbury is a

232

gentle person of some culture and he does not have the political strength in his ward (the Thirtieth) or in the city that his neighbor Magistrate Henry possesses. This is partly because the "Judge" is a younger man and a skilled campaigner. He has a superior flair for winning votes. He is Grand Treasurer of the Colored Elks of the United States as well as head of the Philadelphia Colored Elks lodge. He is a darker and smaller edition of Senator James Davis of Pennsylvania.

Asbury was nominated at the primary but finished last among the nominees in the final election. Henry won the nomination of the new Town Meeting party and that of the rejuvenated Democratic party although he lost the Republican nomination. In the final vote his name led all the rest. He was high man in a field of sixteen victorious candidates. This was largely because he was the nominee of two popular parties, but his name was a factor too. Again Vare erred in alienating needed support.

Dave Hart wanted his lieutenant John Fox placed on the magistrate's ticket. Vare refused and Uncle Dave went to war. He is seventy-seven years old, and in addition to being one of the most truthful of all the ward leaders he is also one of the most powerful, an old-fashioned leader whose power comes from the people of his ward and not from the overlords of the downtown organization. Unlike that of the majority of the other forty-nine leaders Dave's record is one of wavering loyalty to the Vare organization. Vare should have made a greater effort toward keeping this grand old man from northeast Philadelphia in line. Both in the primary

233

and the election Hart effectively worked against the Republican ticket.

In order to provide for minority representation the Pennsylvania Constitution restricts the voters' choice for certain officials, including magistrates, to two-thirds of those elected. Until 1933 the Republican organization controlled both groups of magistrates through the device of throwing votes. Certain Republican stalwarts would register as Democrats and control the Democratic primaries. The Republicans were unable to do this in 1933 because of the increased bona fide Democratic sentiment. At the election, for the first time since before the turn of the century, the Democrats elected the ten majority magistrates and the Republicans won the six minority places. Furthermore, the four defeated magistrates, Joe Whyte, John DiNero, John C. Asbury, and John F. Rigney, were Vare's men and the successful Republican nominees were followers of the old Penrose-McNichol faction. According to Vare's ward leaders the vote was deliberately manipulated to favor the original Penrose men at the expense of the Vare stalwarts. The magistrate vote was a defeat for the Republicans, but more particularly the Vare Republicans. (The old antagonism between Vare and Penrose seemed to have disappeared after the Big Grizzly's death, but the resulting peace was really no more substantial than that created by the Treaty of Versailles.) The Vare organization did not achieve its strength through the quality of party strategy and political leadership displayed in these 1933 campaigns. And the tactical blunders of these campaigns led to the reorganization of the Republican Central Campaign Committee and the overthrow of Vare, just two months before his death in 1934. There is no reformer so effective as *defeat*. It registers a warning that cannot be liquidated by words.

Sinews of War

In this election the opposition was strong in dollars as well as men. Official statements concerning political contributions and expenditures, however, are relative rather than exact, and this is true of all parties that have a chance of winning. Last winter a prominent Progressive was talking to me about his benefactions to the party in Wisconsin, but, when I urged him to say exactly how much he had contributed, he closed the discussion with, "Now you know that the law is strict out here, but we always spent as much as we needed to spend to win. I can't say how much, now; why burn the bridge behind you?" And a leader of the Independents in the Republican Alliance fight of 1929 in Philadelphia referred to their official financial statement as "Stinko." It just happens that I know the exact amount of money provided by the Republican Central Campaign Committee in November, 1933, for one of Philadelphia's fifty wards. I find that comparing this actual figure with the amount officially reported for this ward is like comparing three and one-half with one; so again I say that officially reported receipts and expenditures are likely to be relative rather than absolute.

According to the reports on file in the Clerk of Quarter Sessions' office in City Hall, the Republican party

235

received $104,075.03 and expended $105,796.98 in this election. The official Democratic City Committee under the discredited O'Donnell leadership received $9,035.67 and expended $6,188.08; the Independent Democratic Committee (*i.e.*, the newly organized Democratic party) received $25,977.11 and spent $24,643.98. A group of Republicans opposed to the Vare leadership campaigned under the name of the Town Meeting party. They received $29,658.97 and spent $29,633.97. Of course it is meaningless to attempt to find out the comparative amounts expended by the different parties in a campaign without assigning some weight to the fact that a great majority of Republican committeemen are on the public pay roll and many of these individuals campaign the year round through the personal services that they provide for the voters. This fact further emphasizes the strength and amount of Democratic sentiment when the balloting was done, for, in spite of the expenditure of lesser amounts of money and energy, the Democrats won because they were going with the tide.

Again referring to the official expense account, I find that the money was expended largely for watchers (*i.e.*, party workers) and messengers, at $5.00 or $10.00 each. Other items were rent, postage, printing and stationery, and clerical help, and a few of the wards reported decorations and parades.

The Press

Both the press and, to a lesser extent, the radio helpfully contributed to the formation and direction of opinion in the campaign. All the big daily newspapers

236

reported political meetings and campaign speeches fully, but no newspaper was so powerful as the revitalized and rapidly growing *Record*. The *Daily News*, a tabloid newspaper, strongly supported the Vare ticket; the *Philadelphia Inquirer* supported the Republican candidates almost as strongly as did the *News;* the *Public Ledger* and the *Evening Public Ledger* devoted much space to a discussion of the campaign and mildly supported the Republicans; the *Evening Bulletin*, the newspaper of greatest circulation (499,724) and most like traditional Philadelphia, maintained a more independent attitude during the campaign, although it, too, was more Republican than Democratic; while the *Record* not only gave much space to the campaign and related questions, but most vigorously and effectively attacked the Republicans and supported the Independent Democrats. And although its circulation is only about one-fifth that of the five Republican papers, it exerted so powerful an influence through its editorial and news columns and cartoons that it may be counted as one of the important reasons why the organization met with defeat.

The *Record* successfully reflected the prevailing sentiment of the people, and for this reason its influence was far greater than the extent of its circulation might indicate. It is a rapidly growing newspaper—Democratic, liberal, and semi-sensational. It is often a crusader for lost causes, but this time it was on the winning side. It has Jerry Doyle, Philadelphia's only effective cartoonist and one who approaches Rollin Kirby in pictorial skill. He devoted his talent to the local campaign, and

237

his vivid drawings pointed the gist of the *Record's* editorials and news items and often served as a capstone for both. A typical cartoon shows Vare in a check suit on the driver's seat of a garbage truck. A plaid figure to represent Big Business is spraying perfume on the garbage, Mayor Moore standing alongside, megaphone to his mouth, shouting, "Com' on Folks, Plenty of Seats on the Band Wagon!" while a hypothetical Philadelphia voter is holding his nose and waving the truck invitation aside. Another cartoon revealed John O'Donnell (then Chairman of the discredited Democratic City Committee) and William S. Vare in overalls with paste bucket and brush standing before a huge poster that they had just put up. The poster bears a picture of a great black eagle with wings outspread; the eagle is holding the donkey in one claw and the GOP elephant in the other. Across one wing are the words "Vare-O'Donnell Alliance." At the bottom of the cartoon is the statement, "We Do Our Part-Y." On election day Doyle's cartoon pictured the leaders on the Republican ticket draped in robes and sitting at a banquet table. Vare is seated at the head of the table. The group is startled by the appearance of a phantom hand of the Philadelphia Voter making an X opposite the word "Democratic" on the wall. Below are the ominous words "The Days of Thy Kingdom Are Numbered, And It Is at an End."

The most telling appeal carried by the *Record* covered four columns from top to bottom of its front page of October 30. The upper half contained a photograph of Vare's palatial Atlantic City home, with Vare and two members of his family in an inset, under the caption:

238

"The Top of the Political Machine." Below is another picture under the words "and the Bottom." A negro man, woman, and two children are huddled about a small oil stove in a dingy room. There follows a description of the negro family's plight, which is briefly given in two heavy lines: "Harvey Harman (Ashman) Couldn't Pay $4 'Assessment' So Vare's Machine Kicked Him out of His $11-a-week Job."

On November first the *Record* carried "A Photostat Editorial" on its front page. First of all was a photostat of a letter sent to a given judge (presumably all of the judges in the Common Pleas Courts) by James M. Hazlett, Recorder of Deeds. The letter was a request for an appointment of a mastership for B. B. De Young. Below in heavy black type was an explanatory statement, excerpts of which follow:

The Philadelphia Record charged yesterday that the Vare Organization pays its private debts out of public funds. . . . James M. Hazlett, who asked the Judges to give a job to De Young, is not only Recorder but Chairman of the Republican City Committee.

When you get a letter from Jim it is an order from the Vare high command. Vare has always expected his judges to appoint the people he wants, even to Masterships.

Every Mastership means a $100 fee. Enough Masterships and Mr. Merchant's debt to Mr. De Young will be paid.

In a lengthy article appearing three days later the *Record* charged Vare waste with dragging the city to the brink of ruin.

Philadelphia's indebtedness today is approximately $575,-000,000. It is costing the taxpayers of this city $32,000,000

239

annually to meet the interest and sinking fund charges on outstanding bonds floated for the most part during the last twenty years. The funded debt has been pyramiding in amazing fashion since the political ascendancy of Boss Vare. . . . The survey revealed that "a Bureau of Bosses" costs the taxpayers of Philadelphia $8,000,000 a year. The "Bureau" was the Vare organization. Its colossal cost represented city salaries paid to ward leaders, Vare henchmen and hangers-on.

The *Record* supported the Democratic candidates for City Controller and City Treasurer as strongly as possible. In the above article it said,

Time and again, Hadley as Controller and Wilson as his then deputy, stood shoulder-to-shoulder in a "they shall not pass" stand against padded payrolls, crooked municipal contracts, the atrocious $149,000,000 P. R. T. underlier deal. . . .

Many people, probably a great majority that were suffering from the depression, felt that they were not being efficiently and economically governed. During the past, in days of prosperity, they had given less thought to the way in which their municipal affairs were managed; now, in the time of stress, the people turned their attention to public affairs; and the *Record* provided pertinent materials for thought.

The Radio

For the first time in its history the organization turned to the radio in support of local candidates. Early in the campaign small stations, later larger ones, were used in biweekly talks. Mayor Moore was the organization's most effective speaker. In two addresses he made strong

240

pleas for the election of the entire Republican ticket, and the brunt of a bitter attack was directed at the candidates for City Treasurer and City Controller, WillB Hadley and S. Davis Wilson. The Mayor said that the election of these two officials would endanger his economy program, and, since the more conservative voters think of their Mayor as a second Coolidge, his words carried weight. They changed votes, but not enough to enable the Republicans to win. The *Record* answered the attack with a front page editorial: "Mayor Moore Pays in Advance for the Governorship."

The Democratic party and the newly preempted Town Meeting party relied more largely on the radio than did the organization. Ben Golder, criminal lawyer and former Congressman, delivered some addresses that proved as deadly politically as machine-gun fire. To mention the outstanding example, Golder's bitter and well-founded attack on Merchant forced Merchant off the ticket after he had won the nomination for City Controller, caused an investigation by the school board into the irregularities of Merchant, their secretary, in the purchase of real estate, and finally led the Board of Public Education to dismiss or retire Merchant on a pension. Golder's attacks and the investigation and hearings were front-page news in all the papers.

The campaign, whether centering on radio addresses, newspaper appeals, or face-to-face talks, revolved around the offices of City Controller and City Treasurer. The other offices, save the judges, were carried with the tide; candidates for these offices were carried with the tide, too, only they helped make the tide. The issue

241

in the campaign was in essence the New Deal under the Roosevelt democracy or the Old Deal under Vare. This is one campaign in Vare's history when his endorsement was fatal. Vare had rejected both Hadley and Wilson and, although they had run under the Republican banner in the past, this time they stood as nominees of a new Democratic and new Town Meeting party.

The Future

The future of the Republican party in Philadelphia and in the rest of the forty-eight states is uncertain. Its best argument for victory—prosperity—is wanting. Furthermore, the Democratic party, nationally, has bestowed material favors on so grand a scale and so persistently that the Republican ward politician's campaign cry of "Service" is all but engulfed in the ever flowing rivers of services from the Federal government. And where one appears to be a gift, the other has all the characteristics of a steady income. Will Rogers used the happiest figure of speech I know when he said, "As powerful as a Democrat with a treasury behind him!" The popularity of the Democrats, nationally, has vitally helped them locally, in Philadelphia, and elsewhere. Later, when the danger is less imminent, and the costs are more apparent, the public mind may change. It is also true that the local Democrats cannot forever live in reflected glory, or always win because the party of the opposition has governed wastefully in the past. In spite of the fact that the electorate is becoming increasingly interested in its officials, the favorable results of this new interest are not yet clearly apparent.

One of the Democrats elected to an important county office in Philadelphia in 1933 has already refused to keep a campaign promise that he turn over to the city all fees coming to his lucrative office in excess of $10,000. Several of the Democratic magistrates have been seriously reprimanded by the higher courts for carelessness, or worse, in administering their functions. The Democratic victory in 1933 was sudden, and perhaps for this reason the candidates selected were not substantially different from their predecessors. There will be a real contest in 1935, when a mayor and city councilmen are to be chosen. At that time it may be that the merits of the individual candidates will have more to do with their success or failure at the polls than has been the case in the Quaker City for many years.

The Republican party's future depends on the wisdom of its leaders and their ability to formulate a program and to endorse candidates suited to the new needs of a new electorate. In one sense, 1929 marked the end of an era not only in finance but in politics; it is probably true that the public officials of the future will be more interested in the common good than they have been in the past. But there is a social lag and it may take several defeats before a leadership of civic vision and moral courage is established. And of course it can never come, or it cannot survive the acid test of the ballots after it does come, if the new leadership does not receive the enlightened cooperation of the people. I say *cooperation* rather than *support* because a political leader—unlike angels and archangels—does not exist apart from men and affairs. He is a natural phenomenon, not a legal

243

device; and he is a prototype of his people, not a "sport" or a freak; he is one of them. In fact, in viewing a politician that has been representing the people for ten, twenty, thirty, or more years, I have often felt that I was seeing his constituency in miniature—not all of it, but its basic quality. In normal times he is the expression of the general tenor of his people. If they, the voters, are primarily politicians in attitude, if they are not essentially interested in social justice, but rather seeking some special advantage, some private favor, then the politician must continue to be what he has been in the past, for the politician in the United States is the voter writ large. This is one of the results of our democracy. Therefore, if the electorate is enough interested in its own welfare to know and support the leaders who serve a public purpose, and to refuse support to those who do not, the successful political leaders will be individuals of social vision and moral courage; this follows as the night the day.* It may be that the king's mistress should

* An editorial *It Can Be Done* in the Feb. 25, 1935, *Chicago Daily News* is so directly on this point that I quote part of it here.

"Corrupt elections, perverted civil service, public-works graft, pay-roll plunder, politico-underworld alliances, protected crime and rackets—all these things Chicagoans know from experience; all these things decent Chicagoans deplore. The citizens of Cincinnati once experienced and deplored them. City Manager Dykstra tells us that Cincinnati knows them no more. He says they have been driven from the big city on the banks of the turbid Ohio.

"It can be done, he says.

"In Cincinnati, with a tax rate of $16.86 per $1,000—said to be the lowest in any city in America—a dollar of revenue brings a dollar's worth of service. It pays for good streets and clean streets, for adequate lighting, for the maintenance of public property, for health and safety. The taxpayer gets what he pays for, and pays for nothing more.

"It can be done. . . .

244

not be condemned more than the king; and if this be true, then any indictment or criticism against the majority of politicians is, *ipso facto*, an equal rebuke to the people. As I have said, Depression is the great reformer. It liquidates wealth, traditions, and opinions. The political leaders who understand that new values are required are in accord with the times and with the people. The depression may interrupt their power but it will not destroy it.

If, however, there is too great a lag on the part of the leader he may be permanently relegated to the rear. And it was this lag, broadly speaking, that caused the stricken Vare's personal defeat in 1934,* and the defeat of the tired Hoover two years earlier.

Of course, in present-day America, there are many and persuasive, if not compelling, rivals for the elec-

---

"In Cincinnati national politics has been eliminated from municipal house-keeping. What the city manager, the mayor or the commissioners think about the New Deal, the gold standard, the tariff or the world court has no bearing on Cincinnati's elections or its municipal appointments. Officials qualify for office on knowledge of the city's problems and fitness to solve them. And Cincinnati has a civil service career system.

"It can be done.

"It is not done in all city-manager cities. It is done in Cincinnati because the citizens, who organized to obtain a city-manager charter, did not make the fatal mistake of assuming that their job was done when they had obtained a new and better mechanism. They remained organized to see that the mechanism was kept in skilled and honest hands. The charter organization is on the job. It has made 'Civic service without pay' a watchword of Cincinnatians. It is prepared when election day approaches. It puts in the field an army of volunteers, trained and capable.

"It can be done."

* I have written at some length about *The End of Vare* in an article for *The Political Science Quarterly*.

torate's attention. These increase as prosperity returns. If the citizen's gaze then wanders from politics, the regulars may again find that the battle—for the immediate present—is over and that the Old, Old Deal is again in order. There can never, for any period of time, be government for the people without government by the people. It must be forever remembered that eternal vigilance is not only the price of liberty—it is also the price of good government. This fundamental fact explains why good government is so rare in our history; it is not that elected public officials are abnormally lacking in virtue and honor.

The Republican leaders in Philadelphia gave some indication of their willingness to provide more efficient municipal housekeeping when the Recorder of Deeds (a ward leader) announced that he was installing a photostat service, thereby saving the city $30,000 a year. The excellent Bureau of Municipal Research had long urged that this be done; but it took a defeat, plus the fear of another defeat, finally to get the Republicans to do it. Economies in Mayor Moore's administration might be mentioned in support of the above idea, but the weight of the evidence for the leaders that rule the city and the organization is that they change slowly, and their first thoughts toward future victory have more to do with perfecting party management than municipal machinery. In the past, ward leaders have died (as a number of them have done in recent years), but they never, or almost never, resign on the eve of an important contest. Yet two members of the Republican City Committee, representing wards thereon that have too

246

often gone Democratic in these last years, handed in their resignation in February. (One of these was a straw boss, or "post-card" leader—*i.e.*, he did the detail work of managing the ward; the big decisions are made by a judge who does not care to be identified with the ward leadership.) This man, like 80 per cent of the other present-day ward leaders, is an *order* man: he resigned to escape from being dethroned by the leadership at the top. In this case it is simply a change in the business managership of the ward as opposed to the real leadership. The other leader is stronger, but he is not one of the strong leaders. His health is bad and the times are nerve destroying. He was going to step down for a younger man. However, the members of his ward committee have petitioned him to remain, and he will accede to their wishes for the present. More than a third of the committeemen in still another ward have just asked the City Committee to remove their leader because he does not live in his ward and neglects its best interest.

Since the 1933 defeat there has been, and still is, much talk and rumor of change. The Young Republicans are more active now, giving luncheons, talking, planning, but the Old Republicans are still in the saddle. In spite of the younger group and an increased activity and interest on the part of the women, the older leaders are, with few exceptions, likely to remain in control, particularly if the Republican party avoids defeat this year. Even the probe by the Bar Association and the subsequent citing for trial before five Common Pleas judges of eight attorneys for professional misconduct will probably not destroy the political influence (although it may check it) of one of these eight who is both a state Senator and a very shrewd and powerful ward leader.

Whether or not Philadelphia is governed in the future by the Republican party or the Democratic party, it will probably be governed by an organization—or possibly by two competing organizations. There have been other successful revolts against the organization before; the 1905 campaign is a notable example. But the most interesting result of the citizens' victory then was not to change the nature of politics but to enhance the prestige of the Vares.*

Kings and bosses die, but the institutions and systems requiring kings and bosses live on; although kingdoms as well as kings have been destroyed in Europe since democracy was established in America; and although more recently, since the World War, both the kingly office and its royal occupants have been abolished in Russia, Germany, Spain, to mention only a few out-

* The victors in the 1905 contest were led and largely supported by a group of independent, nonorganization citizens who first organized a Committee of Seventy. And though this group received political help, it was a more homogeneous combination of individuals than was the winning majority in 1933. Following the earlier defeat there were many expressions of jubilation by citizens and press. I select one from the *Public Ledger* of November 9, 1905, which is descriptive of many: "This is the end of it. It was the greatest political machine ever constructed and for a generation it has ground out but one kind of grist. It could not be put together again now, even if there were any man competent to attempt it. The machine is ruined in Philadelphia; it is beaten in Allegheny; it has gone to pieces throughout the State. The attempt to elect Plummer to the treasury in the interest of bank wreckers, joined with the attempt to restore the power of McNichol and Company here, was the last convulsive throb of a dying dynasty. With its death Philadelphia begins a new chain of political history."

standing examples—and not to refer to Italy and other countries where revolutionary changes have taken place. Here in the United States the city of Cincinnati over-whelmingly repudiated what had been long considered a powerful political machine, and, most amazing, substituted in place of the fallen Hynicka an organized and alert citizenry. This newly awakened interest in the common good on the part of a controlling number of citizens is the only substitute for the rule of a boss. The people of Cincinnati have demonstrated their possession of this interest in four successive municipal elections. This phenomenon is rare, and that is the reason why the Cincinnati experiment is heralded so widely. The majorities of the candidates of the Cincinnati Charter Committee, however, are growing smaller, and, if the people neglect their political duties, neither Murray Seasongood, Henry Bentley, nor George Washington can prevent a group of professional politicians from regaining the lost city; for Cincinnati, like other American cities, is a democracy. The significant fact to remember in considering monarchical government in Europe and party organization in great cities is not the king or party boss and his virtues and vices, but the nature of the institutions. It is a system that confronts the people, not an individual.

※※※※※※※※※※※※※※※※※※※※※※

IV
A CONCLUSION
AND
A FORECAST
●

※※※※※※※※※※※※※※※※※※※※※※

A Conclusion and a Forecast

>>>->>>->>>->>>->>>->>>->>>->>>->>>->>>->>>(((-(((-(((-(((-(((-(((-(((-(((-(((-(((-(((

THE voter in the Great Society of today is confronted by an equation between an economic situation and a political situation. Human nature is a constant, and people generally will act in accord with what they believe to be their interest. Those who do not vote are of the opinion that they cannot helpfully modify their political-economic situation by casting a ballot on election day. Those who do vote with faith that they can thereby improve their political-economic situation may roughly be classified into two groups; the pro- and the anti- organization voters.

The latter group contains a preponderant number of individuals who tend to be intellectually independent, economically secure, and socially stable. They are able to manage their own affairs; they are law abiding and gainfully employed; they have enough imagination and social vision to enable them to see beyond the boundary lines of their division and ward; their political judgments are not ready-made by a ward politician, but are a composite of their own opinions plus what they read in newspapers, periodicals, and books, and hear over the radio or from lecture platforms and other forums; and they are the groups that most often respond to

253

intangible ideals, principles, and social objectives. They are largely members of the middle class rather than of the capitalist or proletariat groups. Their influence in politics, however, has been weakened by their lack of effective leadership and organization, and, in Pennsylvania, where the organization is Republican, by their traditional Republicanism. Their loyalty to the Republican banner has led them, in normal times, to support candidates that they might otherwise have opposed. Though they were the first to vote against the organization candidates in the great depression, yet in times of prosperity they have either voted for the nominees of their party, refrained from voting, or weakened their strength by scattering their votes.

The pro-organization voters are largely those individuals with an incarnate want, a need that the party organization can satisfy, or seem to satisfy. Their dependence may be the result of an insecure economic position due to such things as a language or tradition handicap, a failure to observe laws and ordinances, a faulty social education, or a general inability to manage their own affairs. To them the official government is remote,* and the party organization is a human service institution that they support in exchange for personal service, or because a friend asks them to and they have no strong reason for denying the request. They live in various parts of their cities, but are found in greatest numbers in the older sections. Here politics is primarily a business,

* Again I wish to say that in times of economic adversity and a radio, a President Roosevelt or a Senator Huey Long may cause that which ordinarily seems remote to appear alive and vivid.

and as head of that business the division leader is, in the majority of elections, the embodiment of all things political and governmental. Personal contacts count mightily, and secondary appeals not at all. Authority rather than freedom of discussion is here the mainspring of political action, and the atmosphere in some of these bailiwicks resembles Mussolini's Italy rather than democratic America. It is only in times like the fourth year and after of the great depression that this core of the organization's strength weakens. These normally faithful voters finally protest because their economic situation has gradually been adversely affected beyond the power of the party organization to make it up to them.

An important section of the capitalist and upper middle class may also support the dominant organization because they favor the *status quo;* or they hope for special privileges from the official government— privileges which range from tax exemption or tax reduction for a railroad, or a special contractual arrangement for a gas company or other public utility, to the accepted right of a small merchant to use part of the sidewalk space in front of his place of business for his own purposes.

In addition there are substantial numbers of people, more in times of prosperity than in periods of economic adversity, who do not care to participate in the management of public affairs even to the extent of thoughtfully marking a ballot. These individuals are found in all classes of the population and are by no means restricted to the working class. Political morality is not an inevitable feature of high civilization, as Clive Bell has pointed out. The most civilized people in a city like Philadelphia may prefer to live peacefully under the Vares, provided the cost is not too great, than fretfully under the LaFollettes. During the period when civilization had reached its highest pitch in Italy, political methods had fallen to very low levels. Though the art of government is difficult, fascinating, and of high importance, and though some of the greatest figures in history have devoted their lives to it, other great personalities have preferred to act as though they were subjects instead of citizens. They have been seemingly unmindful of the governing process of which they were a part; literature, painting, science, music, or business have absorbed all their attention, and their inactivity has been a definite source of strength to the politician.

At present the attitude of those who have habitually supported the professional politicians is radically changing toward the official government as the result of the dramatic leadership of President Roosevelt and his New Deal program. Formerly the government was one of the things in life that did not matter, or was something to circumvent, but now in the face of their greatest need it appears as a social agent of enormous potentialities. No more can a division leader say to a hesitant voter at election time, "What has Roosevelt ever done for you?" because today the rank and file of the voters believe that Roosevelt has done something for them, and exactly at a time when their need was greatest and their division leader was powerless to help. Therefore,

256

when they voted Democratic in 1933, they acted according to the principle in politics that has always guided their voting, the *service* principle.

The present marks, then, as I have said, a transition in the attitude of American public opinion toward the role of government in our daily life. The advent of the great depression has destroyed even lip service to the Jeffersonian doctrine that that government is best that governs least. In its place is the general conviction that the best government is the one that most helpfully serves the people. So long as the great depression continues, that is, so long as private initiative proves inadequate, the government will stand, if it stands at all, as a servant of the people; and this will enhance the significance of the ballot for citizens striving to maintain their equilibrium in the political-economic society in which they live.

President Roosevelt, on March 3, 1934, delivered an address at the American University in which he pointed out what, in his opinion, was "one of the most salient features . . . in our American life" during his first year in the presidency. He said, "I speak of the amazing and universal increase in the intelligent interest which the people of the United States are taking in the whole subject of government." He stressed in his speech what every seeing person has noted—a change in the typical attitude of the twentieth century citizen toward his government that may have social and political implications more far reaching than would the overturn of a monarchy or the setting up of a republic. It marks the birth of something new in our time, a political awareness among the people generally. There are many people "government conscious" today who never before gave government a thought.

This dawning spirit of social responsibility in government is enlarging the real electorate more than did the Nineteenth Amendment. For now the basis of politics is shifting. The citizen's view is being reoriented; he is thinking of a public official rather than a mere party leader. He is looking for social action on the part of the government rather than an individual favor from a politician. The middleman, the party worker, the human equation in politics counts for less and a public official counts for more. He is the object of the voter's attention.

The great depression and the unusual activity of the Federal government, dramatized by the personality of Franklin Roosevelt, are the reasons for the electorate's new interest in public affairs. In December, 1933, Mr. Harry Hopkins, chief of the Emergency Relief Administration and the C.W.A., told a Congressional Committee that there were four million persons on civil works. At the end of Roosevelt's first year in office there were more than 21,500,000 obtaining their livelihood from the government. This means that approximately one out of six citizens is "living on the government," and the end is not in sight. However, instead of attempting to state the specific number of individuals concretely helped by the Federal government either by jobs or loans or gifts of money, it might be most revealing to quote President Roosevelt's statement of recovery costs that is found in his budget message to Congress, Jan. 7, 1935. He there points out that from Feb. 1, 1932 to Nov. 30, 1934, the Federal government expended for recovery and relief $8,164,900,000. This expenditure has been distributed approximately as follows:

Agricultural aid	$1,337,300,000
Relief	2,783,000,000
Public works	1,226,200,000
Aid to home owners	306,300,000
Reconstruction Finance Corporation	2,351,200,000
Miscellaneous	160,900,000

The President goes on to explain that for the above period of less than three years provisions for recovery and relief through appropriations and authorizations reached a grand total of $14,402,400,000. Regardless of the fate of President Roosevelt's work-relief bill that calls for nearly five billion dollars, which is probably the greatest single appropriation in the history of the world, enough has already been written into the record beyond recall to support the statement that the Federal government is directly affecting the individual and family welfare of every man, woman, and child in America. In view of the unprecedented need of the people and the correspondingly great and unprecedented action on the part of the Federal government, and, to a lesser extent, of the state and local governments, and the further fact that the President and hundreds of newspapermen have painstakingly worked to describe, to advertise, to dramatize the nature and significance of what the government is doing for the people; in view of all of this, it is not odd, but inevitable, that the American voter should on his side become interested in his government. The

President's smile is common to all classes; his voice over the radio saying, "Among our objectives, I place the security of the men, women, and children of the nation first," is persuasive and, in many cases, compelling. The voter is sometimes enough of a realist to give his attention to those things that really matter to him. The voter knows, or he will know, that private interests never fail to give their full attention to the government that acts on them and this is the chief reason why our government in the past has often dealt so handsomely with private interests. A government for the people must be by the people, for, if the great electorate does not speak for itself, no one will speak for it. If President Roosevelt, or any other official interested in serving the public, were standing alone without the support of an aroused citizenry he would be powerless, Roosevelt, during the first part of his term at least, understands this paramount fact and therefore he carries his own message to Garcia.

This new attitude toward the ballot will also strengthen the efforts of the increasing number of citizens who seek to introduce new values into their city government, for city government like the national government will be seen to perform economic functions that directly affect the life of every citizen.

Up to this time most of our election laws have let the voter depend on his own judgment, have taken it for granted that he will be honest and informed, without definitely trying to supply him with adequate motives or understandable aims, and without making it seem worth his while to be honest, or to give thought to the

260

problems confronting him. Too little has been done to bring the issues within the limits of the voter's attention; and this has been necessarily so, since the political-economic equation has been stated in terms beyond the comprehension of the majority of voters. But with this new economic relation between the official government and the citizen the motive is provided for a new attitude toward government; the aims of government and the immediacy and significance of these aims become clear to the voter, and hence there is a new incentive for formulating issues that the voter can judge. His attention is fixed on his ballot and his government, not because it is his birthright or because of any spiritual awakening, or other abstract principle, as a rule, but merely because the voter will understand that he can best serve himself by painstakingly supporting an adequate governmental program.

At the same time that the objects of government are being brought within the voter's immediate attention there is developing an increased incentive for strengthening the mechanics of government. Certain changes to this end have been and are now being sponsored by groups of citizens who are interested in bettering their municipal governments. Among the members of these groups, it is needless to say, are individuals of the highest character, ideals, and intelligence. Under the conditions of the new situation, as I see it, these men will be better able to make their views available to the less intelligent members of the electorate. And, although governmental devices are not so meaningful as human attitudes, yet in a larger sense the two are related

261

to the central question of men's influence on public affairs.

It will be increasingly expedient then to clarify the devices of the ballot and the machinery of the government to enable the voter to grasp the political-economic equation which confronts him when he goes to the polls.

There are certain legal arrangements that might well be embodied in the framework of municipal governments generally. Although the specific recommendations that follow refer to Philadelphia as a concrete illustration, their application is general rather than limited to one city. They embody the findings of the best minds in the municipal field; and an examination of the charters of any given city would indicate to what extent the following suggestions are applicable in its particular case.

First of all, there should be city and county consolidation. The area of the city and county are coterminous and should be presided over by one local government, for in order to have what the voter can understand we must have a single responsibility. The existence of a county government confuses public opinion and creates useless expense. The present arrangement strengthens the party organization, but weakens the political party and the city.

Then the law permitting assistance to voters should be abolished, for it can never be fairly administered; and a literacy test provided by educational authorities might well be required, since a person who can neither read nor write is not likely to have an opinion that will be of social value concerning public questions. Also, permanent registration will reduce the voter's burden and strengthen his position; since we assume that, when the voter really sees the part that his vote plays in creating a better social and economic life for himself and his family, he will be more interested than he has been before in fulfilling his obligation to vote. Permanent registration will foster this voting interest by reducing the incidental burden on the elector. Another improvement would be the introduction of the short ballot so that the electorate will be able to mark its own ballot without the assistance or guidance of an expert marker. This will mean that only those offices shall be elective that are significant enough to capture the voters' attention—in short, policy-determining officials plus the city controller! This will enable the voter to fix responsibility on those actually responsible for what the government does. And this group of officials will be small enough to be within the vision of the majority of voters. The voter then might prepare himself for the election with a reasonable amount of effort and not be forced to rely on someone else's opinion or vote a straight party ticket. The constitution should be amended to provide for the appointment of election officers. At present these very important officials are in theory elected, but in actuality they are often appointed by the ward committeeman. The adoption of a city-manager charter and proportional representation might also have far-reaching effects. The city-manager charter will increase the visibility of the actions of public officials. It will help the interested public support those officials

263

who are serving the public good. There is nothing so important as this, for it will strengthen right public actions and check others. Proportional representation is strongly recommended, for it will help each individual feel that his vote is significant. It will increase the effectiveness of a ballot by enabling a voter to say, "A is my first choice for council, but if he does not need my help in order to get elected or if he cannot win with my support, then I want to vote for C or F or some other candidate." The citizen will mark as many choices as he actually has; he will vote for someone rather than against a person that he does not like. This will substitute a positive attitude for one of negation or defeatism. It will cause a member of a minority party or faction to feel that he can vote his first choice without throwing his ballot away. The significant point is that the use of this ballot of higher potentialities will help bring the citizen to the polls, because he will know that he will be able to express his opinion when he gets there. Finally, there is an urgent need for an effective merit system—one that will encourage the most gifted young people in our universities to think of public service as a permanent career—an employment system that recognizes ability, industry, and loyalty (loyalty to the municipal service); a system that will provide security of tenure comparable to that enjoyed by members of the English Civil Service, or found in our most far-seeing private industries. Since administration is the very heart of government, a permanent administrative service is essential to the adequate functioning of municipal affairs. There is also another reason why it is

264

essential. If jobs are not given as rewards for service to the party organization, it will be more easily possible for municipal employees to give their loyalty and best efforts to a city instead of to a party organization. The organization in turn will be forced to rely more on intangibles in politics, and this should be fortunate for every one who is primarily interested in the public good.

In connection with this matter of devices for better government there is one other question of importance which I can only hint at here. It is part and parcel of Lippmann's books on public opinion and is the core of Norman Angell's *The Public Mind*. I refer to an educational training for the citizen, which will better enable him to understand the importance of his vote and to distinguish political truth from political error. As Norman Angell so well says, we have provided our people with a grammar of language; we must now equip them with a grammar of truth or evidence.

The American voters, in times of prosperity, tend to think of their public officials more or less as the people of an earlier day thought of the court fools or jesters in the lives of Shakespeare's kings. But this is only in politics, for in business the employer votes with an aim to select a person of ability and probity. One might then ask why the same individual may act like a child in politics but like an adult in the world of finance. The reason is that we have an inadequate social education for our citizenry.

It is perhaps not so much an "inadequate" as a "faulty" social education. Here in the United States

265

free education for people in every social class and from the nursery to the grave has been increasingly provided in an unprecedented manner. The electorate is so convinced of the social importance of education that in about 80 per cent of the cities the school board is independent of the official city government for fiscal support. The expenditures for other municipal services are determined in the light of the total tax burden, but education is usually permitted to speak for itself. Therefore the weakness is due to the quality or kind of educational training rather than the amount. It is reasonable to believe that *training for citizenship* should be the keystone of the arch in an educational system supported by public taxation, and in a country irrevocably committed to universal suffrage. The Founding Fathers intended it to be; the most lowly taxpayer will endorse the soundness of the idea. But for some reason American education has almost missed this point, and has been concerned with every other conceivable subject, ranging from the syntax of Beowulf or the implications of cube root to what is wrong with the Polish Corridor. Foundations and individuals provide untold sums for research in the fields of industry and medicine, but the fields of citizenship, government, and politics have been conspicuously neglected. One need not question the rightness of the expenditure of time and money in the investigation of the cause and cure of cancer in an individual citizen, in order to believe at the same time that an examination into the nature of a cancer in the body politic is incontestably more important. There are experts daily engaged in providing the myope with tools

266

to increase his vision, but the myopic citizen in politics has not been equipped with any tool to enable him better to distinguish truth from error. Again it is suggested that the astigmatism of democracy also merits the attention of specialists.

Taking up once more the social, economic, and political factors of the city of the future, anyone who writes of it, no matter how sketchily, is dealing with imponderables, the nature or implications of which he cannot foresee, since even the shrewdest politician cannot see beyond the next election. However, the history of municipal government in the United States does make clear that the individualistic formula of laissez faire has been abandoned—"a cold arid thing in the face of living demands for new services." And as cities have grown in population they have grown in per capita expenditures, and their growth in expenditures indicates, in a measure, their increase in municipal functions, in new services to the people.

The most inescapable foundation for the development of a distinctive city spirit is a city government with municipal functions so significant and useful that the citizen associates the city with the maintenance of his individual and family welfare. This more socialized city will count for more in the public mind of the future because the citizen will more directly feel the cost of the government in taxes and its value in social and economic services.

Of course, any increase in the functions of the official government will mean an increase in the tax burden. For example, instead of a tax rate of $1.75 per $100 of assessed valuation as it is today in Philadelphia,* there will be a tax levy of possibly two or three times this much. (And probably this greater tax will be levied on income rather than on real estate.) The significant fact to the citizen, however, would be, not the size of the tax obligation but the value of the goods and services received. Either the increased usefulness of the government or the greater tax burden (particularly if the tax were direct and of a non-shiftable variety) will strengthen the citizen's concern over public matters. His vote will assume a new importance, not because his forefathers fought for it, but because its intelligent use can affect the citizen's life and destiny in a profound manner.

(Of course the entire electorate will not react to the increased services and the correspondingly increased tax burden in the same manner. Those individuals above the disaster level and those hardest hit by the new tax burden with less apparent benefit to themselves will also center their attention on the new social program, but for the purpose of opposing it. In their opposition they will most probably continue to ally themselves with those party organizations committed to the Old Deal. Therefore the division between the "haves" and the "have nots" will become increasingly apparent in future years.)

But to return to our future city—the city of tomorrow that may exist, in point of time, say twenty-five years from today. There is a social lag; material conditions change more rapidly than does the attitude of human

* The school-district tax is not included here.

268

beings. But since the place of government in our daily lives has changed, first from a negative to a neutral force, and then from a neutral to a positive force, and is now becoming the core or jugular vein of our civilization, the attitude of the people toward their government is changing.

The *general* electorate may well become civic-minded for the same reason that a merchant is profit-minded. The citizen will be on the alert for meritorious public service, as well as wastefulness and graft, even as an employer is in the commercial world. This new attitude on the part of the electorate will cause an increasing number of persons with character and ability to contend for public office and these individuals will provide moral leadership for the people in areas that are today neglected.

The functions and probably the character of the regular in politics will necessarily change, for the politician will do whatever the voters compel him to. If the voters' standards in social values change, so will his. Then as now, he will be an embodiment of the basic attitude of the people. If the people are educated to think in terms of the common good, so must the politician be. His attention will necessarily be fixed more on public issues than on individual favors. A basket of groceries is of value today; but in the future, the personal gift of groceries will not loom so large in the voter's mind as a living wage and a sense of social security.

In this new society there will be fewer laws; those that are no longer enforced will be scrapped, and those that remain will express the substantial wishes of the people,

269

and not of some peculiar minority. Hypocrisy will count for less; straight thinking for more. The lawbreaker will then rightly be considered the enemy of society and he will be punished without fear or favor. The friendly magistrate who is no longer a ward leader will say, "You are guilty [if the prisoner is guilty beyond a reasonable doubt] and I sentence you, not because I like you the less but because I love the people more." It would be poor politics to gain one or a dozen votes and to lose ten thousand through this personal act against the people.

The great depression has demonstrated the weakness of private initiative and unofficial organizations in the face of the needs of the present; and for this reason it is probable that the city of the future will creatively function to meet more adequately than does the present city the requisites of the individual and his family. This envisioned municipality will provide, or see to it that a person is provided with, adequate housing, light, heat, transportation, medical attention, work, and recreation, as well as adequate schools and the protective services of today. The citizen will then receive as his right from his city what a certain few now obtain from the politician as a favor. This will mark the emergence of a spirit of social responsibility; issues will count more largely than personalities in the citizen's political thinking; and just as once it was glory to be a Roman and now it is an honor to be a man, so may we find that the individual who once gloried in being a Philadelphia Republican may in the future feel his greatest pride in being a citizen of his City, his State, and his Country.

270